About the Author

The author was born in Wolverhampton, into a comfortable, working class background, in 1945. He attended a newly built comprehensive school, which had dedicated teachers and some twenty acres of grounds, providing excellent sporting facilities. He enjoyed outdoor pursuits, including climbing, hill walking and canoeing.

Choosing catering as a second choice career (after the Forestry Commission), he first trained as a chef and later in hotel management in London. Meeting his future wife in Eastbourne in 1965, they were married in 1968, on their return from London. Until his retirement in 2001, the couple owned and managed several businesses in Eastbourne, including hotels and restaurants.

They now live in Herefordshire.

The Baby Boomers

Rod Corder

The Baby Boomers

Olympia Publishers
London

www.olympiapublishers.com

OLYMPIA PAPERBACK EDITION

A CIP catalogue record for this title is
available from the British Library.

ISBN: 978-1-84897-955-0

First Published in 2018

Olympia Publishers
60 Cannon Street
London
EC4N 6NP

Printed in Great Britain

Dedication

To Gill

Chapter One

"Why don't you come to Eastbourne for the summer?"

The question was put to me by Bill, the young assistant manager at the restaurant in Nottingham where I was employed as second chef. Although I had no way of knowing at the time this question, and my subsequent response, would radically change my life.

It was February 1965, and we, the staff, had just been informed that the proprietors of Le Chateau de l'Aperitif, an up-market restaurant, had sold the business to Bernie Inns, an expanding group of steak bars; and although good at what they did, were decidedly not up-market.

As a young chef of nineteen, I commenced work at The Chateau – as it was known locally – on September 1st 1964. I had been very keen to work there as I felt that I could learn a great deal from a restaurant with such a good reputation. A further point was that the salary offered was three times that of my previous position in Shrewsbury. However, apparently it was too good to last. We had all been given notice but told that anyone who wanted to continue with Bernie Inns could do so if they wished. I had no desire to do this as I felt that grilling steaks day in, day out, would not extend my knowledge one iota and besides, the salary on offer was half of what I was presently earning.

I had, therefore, arranged a position in a hotel in Geneva through an agency in London. This was not highly paid but at that time, Switzerland was considered to be the country which offered the best training programme.

Bill, who was originally from Liverpool, had worked in an hotel in Eastbourne during the summer of 1964, prior to coming to The Chateau, and was returning there in April for the season of 1965. He had been in touch with the proprietors of the hotel and they had mentioned that they would be looking to employ a new head chef.

His description of life in Eastbourne was certainly an attraction for a nineteen-year-old whose main raison d'etre in life was girls. Most of my waking hours, and a good deal of my sleep, seemed to dwell on these wondrous creatures that I had discovered in my early teens. Also, if I am honest, probably one of the main reasons that I had moved to Nottingham was because I had read somewhere that Nottingham had a positive plethora of females, a ratio of three or four to each male, no less!

It had certainly proved to be a heavenly city in the few short months that I had been there; this in spite of the obstacle to a social life of not finishing work until ten thirty pm.

But now it was coming to an end and Bill's talk of finishing work in the hotel in Eastbourne at eight thirty to nine pm, sounded almost like being on holiday.

A decision had to be made and after an interview with the Eastbourne hoteliers in London, I cancelled my appointment in Geneva and opted for the south coast.

It was decided that Philip, another friend, would have to move to Eastbourne too, possibly against his will. Philip was a very amusing, witty and outgoing person with an extended fund of jokes, but could not seem to organise his life and was completely useless with money. He owed me the best part of eighty pounds, a small fortune then, and I knew that if I didn't take him with us, I was most unlikely to see its return; and besides, he was the only one with a car.

Philip was already employed at The Chateau when I commenced work there. We quickly became good friends and, as a local lad, he was an entrée into a large circle of new acquaintances. He took a great delight in provoking Tony, the head chef, a volatile Italian. Tony, a relatively young man, had just had a new set of false teeth to which Philip would draw attention by clicking his own teeth together several times after each food order he gave and then grinning like an imbecile. On one occasion, after most of the waiting staff had been told that one of the dishes on the menu (trout) was now finished. Philip came out with an order for trout and accompanied it with his usual teeth chattering, Cheshire cat impersonation. Tony erupted and, picking him up bodily by the seat of his trousers and the scruff of his neck, threw him straight back through the swing doors into the restaurant. At tremendous velocity, but at low level, he happened to end up under the table of the customers from whom he had just taken the order and rolling over said, as nonchalantly as possible, "Trout's off!"

Surprisingly, when the idea of coming to Eastbourne was put to him, Philip seemed quite keen and so it proved unnecessary to abduct him and drive him south in his own vehicle.

As we had been given a month's notice, I decided to leave straight away and rented a bedsitter in West Bridgeford while I was waiting for Bill and Philip, who both needed to continue working for the month.

Early one morning they came round with two girls in tow and having let themselves in, proceeded to make a coffee. I was only vaguely aware that they were there as I was still suffering from the excesses of the night before – a condition that used to be known as crapulous; although, not unsurprisingly this description of a hangover has fallen out of use! I was awoken more fully by coughs and spits and someone (a girl's voice) saying, "What disgusting coffee."

"It's probably something to do with my dirty socks in the kettle," I suggested. "I think you have just boiled them up. The smell was so overpowering last night when I took my shoes off, that it was necessary to put them somewhere enclosed."

Now, being fully awake, I noticed one of the girls, although somewhat pale, no doubt from the thought of what she had just imbibed, was a voluptuous creature with long, auburn hair.

Later that day, Philip asked if I wanted to go to The Kardomah (a coffee bar) with him as he was going to meet Marian, the ravishing girl that he had brought round earlier.

"How long have you been seeing her?" I asked.

"I'm not yet," said Philip. "I'm working on it. She is a bit older than us, twenty-seven, I believe."

"This is Rod," said Philip, introducing me to Marian. "You remember, him of the stinking socks?"

It soon became apparent that Marian wasn't interested in Philip, which was unusual as he usually managed to 'pull' whoever he fancied. This was confirmed when, much to my surprise, and after a couple of sarcastic comments in regard to my somewhat chaotic living arrangements, she suggested that as my bedsitter was a bit of a hovel and it was only about three weeks before we all left for Eastbourne, I could, if I wanted, move in with her. I knew that she lived in a modern block of flats.

"But you only have one bedroom!" yelped Philip!

"That's right," said Marian, "but Rod could always sleep in the lounge if he prefers to!"

Although this was the beginning of the swinging sixties and I thought myself to be a bit of a lad about town, with my long hair, fancy clothes and Cuban-heel boots (the main cause of the state of my socks) I must admit that I was still taken aback somewhat at this uninhibited proposition; but I moved in the next day anyway!

Much to Philip's chagrin, the next three or four weeks were spent in a state of sexual bliss. Marian had the sort of body that I had only dreamed about (frequently) hitherto. Things got even better when she told me that she was bisexual and introduced me to an equally ravishing friend who was as uninhibited as herself. The days, of course, raced by.

A couple of nights before we were due to leave for Eastbourne, we had a farewell party at Marian's which got a little out of hand as about a hundred people turned up, not all invited.

Bill, Philip and I left for the south coast on April 12th, with all our worldly goods crammed into Phil's Mini.

The drive down was uneventful apart from it raining heavily and Philip having no windscreen wipers other than one he kept in the glove compartment 'for emergencies'! We stopped for dinner in the evening at a strange restaurant in Sussex, called Batts, and were accosted throughout the meal by a giant dog which appeared to be of the opinion that as he lived there, was entitled to a fair share of any customer's meal.

We arrived in Eastbourne at nine pm and stayed at the hotel where Bill and I were to commence employment.

Chapter Two
Eastbourne

I liked Eastbourne from the beginning, although there did seem to be a dearth of girls.

We were now living in a house on the beach in Pevensey Bay. The house was owned by a family from Plumpton but was devoid of any furniture and occupied by the son (about our age) who was a scruffy Bohemian but likeable character who went by the name of Denton Brockway.

When we arrived, his only furnishings were a mattress and a storm lamp. However, Bill, Denton and myself, with an eye to business, took over and agreed a rent with Denton's older brother, in return for some furnishings. There were several spare rooms, so we let some of them to four lads from Manchester and two Irish lads from Queen's University, who were all working in Eastbourne during the summer.

These were halcyon days. Philip had found work in a hotel easily enough and I had given it up!

At my interview in London, I had been promised staff that had never materialised and looked as if there were little prospect of them ever doing so. But I had discovered I could work as a relief chef for about six pounds per day and three days' work was sufficient to live on.

After a few weeks, the lack of girls seemed to be acute. I did have a girlfriend but we weren't really suited and in any event, she spent most of her time talking about an ex-boyfriend called Henry, who had ended their relationship. However, I was working on a rather nice hairdresser (one of twin sisters) who I had met in a coffee bar and who had trimmed my hair for me, but as she had a boyfriend there didn't seem much hope. So, a trip to Nottingham was organised, the three of us plus Denton. We arranged to stay with two friends, Wendy and Lyn, but our first port of call was at Marian's flat. I left the other three in the car and went up and knocked on the door. A man's voice shouted, "Who is it?"

I replied that I had come to see Marian. The voice shouted back that she no longer lived there and would I mind f*%&king off as it was three am.

I demanded to know where Marian had moved to and with that the door opened and I was faced by a 'man mountain' in underpants. I felt a blow to my stomach and one to the side of my head and found myself twenty feet away at the bottom of the stairs. I thought it prudent not to go back up. On arriving at Lyn and Wendy's and relating the tale, they said that Marian had been evicted because of the trouble at our leaving party and that 'man mountain' was apparently a heavyweight boxer of some renown, who had taken over her flat.

Mid May

I had fallen asleep on the beach and burned to a cinder.

That same evening I had an interview for a job at a local hotel and, unbeknown to me, a possible date. Philip had mentioned that he and Bill had met two girls, Deane and Gill, Gill being a single mum with a two-year-old daughter. As Philip and Deane had started seeing something of each other, I quite soon met Deane who was a nice-looking, feisty character, but apparently Gill had no interest in Bill.

I had arranged to meet Philip after my interview and he and Deane were going to suggest that they telephone Gill to ask her along. I didn't get the job as I fainted whilst talking to the manager and although I explained that I had fallen asleep in the sun, and had the appearance of a boiled lobster (which must have added some veracity to the story) they obviously thought that I was inebriated. I met up with Philip who was accompanied by Deane and because I looked so ill, they insisted on taking me to hospital, where I was sprayed with something like liquid calamine lotion and then sent home. The next morning I couldn't walk properly.

I spent a week in bed, which gave me ample time to dwell on the fact that not only had I not been offered the job I wanted but even worse, I had missed out on the possibility of a date with the gorgeous Gill. Philip had made things worse by describing her to me and had then informed me that she had started seeing Denton. Perhaps I should have gone to Switzerland after all! However, he did say he would bring her up and introduce us.

During the week I had to stay in bed, we were raided late one night by the Eastbourne police. There had been a robbery in Eastbourne and as we were a group of young lads living in one house, in those innocent days, we were likely suspects. The only thing found was a toast rack from The Cavendish Hotel that one of the lads who worked there had brought in, 'complete with toast', as I was surviving on a diet of sausages on credit from a local butcher. In those days, no work meant no money, it never occurred to anyone that I knew to 'go on the dole'.

The police showed a keen interest in a progress chart that the boys had hung at the bottom of my bed, with such comments as 'Keep your distance, go-no-rrhoea' and 'No effing progress today!'

Although I had asked Philip not to bring Gill to see me, of course he did. I looked a sorry specimen with skin hanging down from my forehead to my nose and wearing specs instead of my usual contact lenses. Fortunately I heard their voices before they came in and so just had time to pick up a newspaper and whip off my specs. The vanity of a nineteen-year-old! The lack of specs meant that I couldn't see Gill, but of course she could see me and no doubt thought what a lucky escape she had had. I mumbled "Hello," on being introduced and then ungraciously studied my newspaper.

Chapter Three
Gill

The next time I saw Gill was about a week later. I had recovered and was lounging flat out on a settee in a room just off the kitchen. I was occupied with my usual thoughts of girls and how to get them and in fact, how to get rid of the one that I had as I was now heartily fed up with 'J' and her incessant bleating about the phantom Henry. It was about ten pm when in strolled Denton followed by this dream (who I could now see), Gill; somewhat French-looking, with short, dark hair and even shorter skirt and high heels. I took all this in with a blink of an eye and then pretended to be asleep. Denton went off to make coffee and Gill sat on the couch opposite me. I opened one eye a fraction and took in as much as I could before she started to look up at me. Clamp, went my eyelid. Wait a few seconds – open fractionally again. She was now replying to something Denton had said from the kitchen. She was facing slightly away from me – so more time to take in this vision of loveliness. She had crossed her legs so that from my horizontal position I could see right up her skirt and was looking at the best pair of legs I had ever seen encased in stockings. Too late, she turned and spotted me; she smiled a merry mischievous smile that lit up her dark, beautiful eyes. She asked me how I was feeling now and said that I looked a lot better than the first time we had met.

Denton came in with coffee, so I sat up as I couldn't legitimately carry on looking at those beautiful thighs, even though I had a sneaking suspicion (later confirmed) that the crossed legs had been for my benefit. The conversation became a little more stilted because each time I looked at Gill, her eyes seemed to hold me and I wanted her more than anything I'd ever wanted before.

End of May

It was almost the end of May and I hadn't seen Gill since that night. I thought about her a lot and kept wondering whether or not I should try to contact her. Philip had told me earlier on that she was seventeen, almost eighteen and that he knew (via Deane) that she had dropped a few hints about me.

Sunday May 30th

One evening, Philip and I went for a coffee in Terminus Road and in walked Deane and Gill. I couldn't believe my luck – although I later found out that they had seen us going into the café. We decided to go for a drink at The Beachy Head Hotel. Gill was now eighteen, it had been her birthday a couple of weeks previously. We talked and were immediately comfortable in each other's company, but with the frisson of excitement of everything to discover about each other intellectually and physically. Gill was amusing with a quick repartee, but also had a warm, friendly and at the same time, endearing personality. I found her tremendously attractive, with a sexuality that I had never seen in another girl. She teased me about pretending to be asleep that last time we met and said she knew I was looking at her legs. I asked if she minded and she replied, "Not at all." We were so engrossed with each other, we almost forgot that Philip and Deane were there and I think that we both knew that we would make love, somewhere, anywhere, that night.

"We're going," said Philip. "Are you two coming or staying here?"

"We're coming," I replied as Philip had the car and it was a long walk down from Beachy Head in the dark.

I started to kiss Gill as we sat in the back of Philip's car and felt her warm body responding and pressing against me. I asked Philip to drop us off at the top of the seafront and then off they drove. "Shall we walk down the lane and look at the sea?" I suggested. Gill agreed. We found a grassy bank, high above the shore near The Sugar Loaf and lay down and started to kiss again. I felt her breasts, firm and responding to my touch. I eased up her skirt to look at those beautiful legs and felt the excitement starting to become overpowering. We made love slowly at first and then hard, forcefully and passionately.

Monday May 31st, 1965

After seeing Gill home, we had arranged to meet the following evening for what was to be our first official date. During what seemed to be an increasingly long day, she was never out of my thoughts and I tried coming to terms with, and even tried unsuccessfully to resist, the all too apparent imbecility which had afflicted me! I attempted to pin down in my own mind what the tremendous attraction that she held for me was. A lot of these attributes, as already mentioned, were obvious. She was very good looking with a wonderful figure, had a lovely personality, was witty with a mischievous sense of humour and her eyes, deep, beautiful, sexy but always smiling and friendly. But there was something else and then I realised that it was charm; she had charm, that indefinable quality that so very few people have. That easy capacity whereby in conversation with someone, they make that person feel that they are the most important thing in their life. I had never met anyone with charm before. That is not to say of course, that everyone that I had met hitherto was charmless (although some were) merely that they did not possess charm.

In the fifty years since our first meeting, I have probably come across two or three others with this quality. I have met several who have tried to be charming and perhaps in some ways they were. However, charm is natural and unforced and I am sure unknown to those who possess it; whereas false charm is unctuous and merely irritating.

That evening we dined out together for the first time, in a small Greek restaurant that we were to use for many years to come. Afterwards, we strolled along the seafront and I knew then that I had met the girl I wanted to be with for the rest of my life

.

Chapter Four
Early Days

I had always loved the countryside and had spent most of my youth walking and cycling in Shropshire and rock climbing and canoeing in Wales. Youngsters were pretty fit in those days – no computers – and on many occasions, a day's cycling would be a sixty to eighty-mile round trip to Ludlow or Church Stretton; well into the Shropshire hills in any event.

I was born in Wolverhampton in 1945, and for the first nine years of my life, lived to the east of the town which seemed to be a long way from any countryside at all. These were years of austerity (rationing continued until 1953) and I remember going with my mother to the Co-op to fetch the rations, never the groceries. However, there is no doubt in my mind that we were the lucky generation. Our parents fought a world war for five or six long years and some of them, World War One too. Austerity would pass and things would get much better by the sixties.

How strange it is, the things that remain in one's mind from childhood. I remember trolley bus trips into town with my mother, where invariably one of the poles would fall off and always there would be the cry from the conductor of 'Any more fares? Pass right down the bus please.'

Another saying – where the memory is accompanied by the feeling of discomfort of cold legs and feet – would crop up when my mother met someone she knew in town, early in the New Year. This always followed the same format. My mother would ask, "Did you have a nice Christmas?"

To which the reply was always, "Quiet, you know."

I always found this fascinating as no one ever said that they had had a busy, or even wild or raucous, festive season. My mother would then lie and say that ours had been quiet too – which it never was, as there always seemed to be tribes of uncles, aunties, cousins and our neighbours trooping in and out. They would continue chatting, seemingly impervious to the cold – it was always snowing – while I had to stand holding my mother's hand, freezing in my short trousers.

Boxing Day was always particularly busy as it was also my parents' wedding anniversary. My father, who never really drank from one Christmas to the next, always poured a teaspoon of whisky into everyone's tea at breakfast. This always seemed such an exciting, outrageous and debauched thing to do – I still keep up the tradition to this day.

I started school at the age of five and very quickly learned to read. Unfortunately, however, within the space of a few months, my eyesight deteriorated quite rapidly. Rather than move me to the front of the class so that I could see the blackboard, it was decided, presumably by the local authority, that I should be moved to a new school, a school for partially sighted children.

The two years spent at this establishment (Graizely) were pretty awful. I had to travel on two buses to get there (on my own) and was supplied with plastic pennies and halfpennies to pay my fare. None of the bus conductors appeared to recognise this currency and very often wanted to turn me off the bus, but were always prevented from doing so by my looking downcast; thereby gaining the support of all the adult passengers. I particularly remember one lady saying to the conductor that he should be ashamed of himself to even consider turning a five-year-old off the bus and how would he feel if it was his child? Having seen the effect that this had, it was a refrain I took up myself quite regularly and would exclaim those exact words in a loud voice, so fomenting a general 'hue and cry' from the rest of the passengers. Eventually I became quite disappointed when my tokens were accepted without question, and I suspect this was the case with many of the regular travellers who had got to know me.

The school was positively Victorian, both in age and in its attitude to teaching. I, along with the other children, was seated at a desk with a gigantic magnifying glass affixed above it. The thinking behind this appeared to be that if a book was placed underneath, on the desk, we would be able to read without the necessity of being taught. Unfortunately, in the two years that I attended this diabolical institution, I was never able to read one printed word, my eyesight was just not that bad, but on no account were we allowed to move the books from under the magnifying glass. Every day was the same. I would be told to commence reading by the teacher, a Mr Treadrer, who was the epitome of the worst type of ignorant bully. Having a vague recollection from my few months of education at my first school, that all stories began 'Once upon a time', which, unfortunately, because of my fear of this apology of a teacher, I now remembered as 'Once a bonner time', this is what I would blurt out.

The reward for this insolence was a smack across the back of the head. This continued two or three times a day for two years but I genuinely never remember him making any attempt at trying to teach me to read.

Eventually it became apparent to my parents that not only was I not learning anything at all but the reading ability that I had acquired at five, had now gone completely. After quite a long and no doubt brave battle on their part with the education authority, I was moved back to my original school where I very quickly caught up.

When I was nine, with great excitement, we moved to a brand new council estate at Finchfield, on the western edge of Wolverhampton. From my bedroom window, I could see real green countryside, something that I had little experience of. Our previous home had an area of scrubby hillocks and a rusty brook half a mile to the east and a Polish refugee camp three or four hundred yards to the west. Apart from this and the East Park, it was mostly houses and factories. My father would, on occasions, point out a brightness in the night sky and told me it was the Northern Lights, but I later found, to my disappointment, that the brightness was in fact from blast furnaces. The Poles in the camp were nice people and would supply us kids with sweets and cigarettes.

The aforementioned scrubby hillocks were, I think, disused mining areas. This was a battleground where we kids from the East Park Estate would meet a tribe from further east (Portabello) and throw bricks and stones at each other across the border – the rusty brook. At the age of five or six, I was used as a secret weapon by my older brother. I would have to walk unseen behind him carrying a large stone and then, as we drew near to the enemy, run out screaming like a banshee and chase them off, hurling the stone at the last straggler. It always seemed to work, they would scatter at a great rate with cries of "He's brought his brother with him!" Amazingly, I never remember anyone getting badly hurt.

An interesting anecdote (at least to me) was that in later life I read several books by a nineteenth century author, George Borrow, his most well-known being *Wild Wales*. As a young man he trained in law but decided it wasn't for him. In his two-book autobiography of his young life, *Lavengro* and *Romany Rye,* he decides to leave London and travel, working his way first by stagecoach and then by foot, across southern England towards Salisbury. Somewhere west of there, he purchases a tinker's horse, cart and tools and sets himself up in the trade. He travels further towards the Welsh border and then swings north east. He meets a Gypsy acquaintance (Jaspar Petulengro) who directs him to a 'good camping place in a dingle', from where he can ply his wares. The dingle is thought to have been situated in Portabello.

George Borrow, although quite an odd character in many respects, was a renowned linguist speaking some fifteen languages, one of them being Romany. The name, Lavengro, – which means 'man of words' – was given to him by his Gypsy friends.

My taste in reading, in my younger days, had been such authors as John Buchan, *Thirty-nine Steps*, *Greenmantle* and *John McNab* et cetera and Walter Scott. I was never interested in science fiction or in fact anything with a hint of mechanics about it. My brother built model aeroplanes and had a Meccano set, which when he eventually gave it to me, I sold! I could never understand the pleasure he appeared to get by building things, rather than sitting down to read a good book. He also, at one stage, had a chemistry set which I found totally incomprehensible. In one of my senior school reports, the space for the chemistry teacher's comment bore the obviously exasperated legend 'He enjoys the films' but even that wasn't true! Later, in my teens, I discovered Dickens, surely the greatest exponent of written English, Thomas Hardy, Trollope and of course many others.

I am still an avid reader and a more contemporary author whose books I think well written is Patrick O'Brian.

Oh, to be able to write as well as the least able of these!

My only experience of the countryside prior to the move to Finchfield, was the annual blackberry expedition. Along with our neighbours, the Pritchards, we would catch a trolley bus into the centre of Wolverhampton and then another bus halfway to Bridgenorth. Here, on the side of a ridge with a wonderful view across Shropshire, we would spend hours picking blackberries followed by a picnic lunch. The children, Terry and Marylyn (my brother and sister) and me, along with Eileen, Raymond and Alan, would have a great time racing about and rolling down the hill. We would catch the bus back about four pm, most of us covered in blackberry juice, but with pounds of blackberries for jam, crumbles and pies, arriving home about five thirty pm in time for what was usually a two family tea.

Finchfield was like a different world compared to the East Park Estate. We were on the edge of the countryside and only a couple of miles from Shropshire. Only a few hundred yards brought us to open fields, a canal, a steam railway and a brook that wasn't rusty.

My new junior school was just around the corner, a modern building with indoor toilets that didn't freeze up in winter. One day we had a visit from Billy Wright, the Wolves and England football captain. He watched us play a match and I couldn't understand why I, as captain of the team (by rote, not merit), wasn't immediately signed up for Wolves Colts.

In 1956, I was due to go to senior school, which was newly built and had opened only twelve months previously. However, sometime in July, I contracted polio – fortunately non-paralytic – and so spent some eight weeks in an isolation hospital. I was extremely fortunate as several of the children in there with me were badly incapacitated and some died. Whilst in hospital, I had a somewhat strange pastime if I was bored; perhaps having used up the week's supply of books and comics. I would time myself to see how long I could hold my breath. With hindsight, this appears to have been quite bizarre behaviour, as parked in my cubicle was the hospital's 'iron lung'; but I was only ten years of age and fortunately never had need of it.

I finally went to the senior school, The Regis, in late September. The Regis School in Tettenhall, a couple of miles away, was one of the first comprehensives in the country. As I have mentioned, it was newly built with building works still in progress. It eventually became a first-rate school with some twenty acres of grounds, which included rugby and football pitches, a quarter mile cinder running track, tennis courts and two gymnasiums. Sport and exercise were of premier importance then, there was no chance of any child becoming obese. Apart from football, rugby, cricket, tennis and athletics, all boys had to take part in a cross country run once a week. Five miles for the younger ones and seven to eight miles when we were older.

The teaching staff, under the headmastership of William Cretney and his deputy, a dour Scot by the name of 'The Dreaded MacGregor'. All wore traditional gowns and were excellent at their jobs, with few exceptions.

Discipline and punishment, administered by The Dreaded MacGregor, was firm and would no doubt be thought of as harsh now, but was also sometimes carried out with a touch of humour. On one occasion, having set off the fire alarms, I was made to guard the one I had activated for a whole week at all breaks and lunchtimes, in case any other boy had a similar urge to evacuate the school! On another, whilst waiting for one of my friends (who was having a pee in the boys' toilets) I managed to direct a stream of water from the drinking fountain in a long and satisfying arc of some ten feet in length, straight onto the back of his head.

The loo door swung open and who should be standing there but The Dreaded MacGregor. Once again I was made to guard that particular fountain for a week, in case anyone else had a similar inclination.

However, serious misdemeanours such as smoking – although, suspiciously, Mac always smelled of tobacco – warranted six strokes of a broken window pole, on whichever hand was not used for writing.

Mac, besides being deputy head, was also head of maths and was so enthusiastic and good at his job that he managed to imbue me with enthusiasm too.

Girls were an intrinsic part of my school days. I can't imagine anything more dull than a boys only school, where one would, on a dreamy afternoon in a French lesson, be unable to gaze with lust and affection at the object of one's desire of the week. This, of course, wasn't necessarily reciprocated!

There was an active outdoor group, boys only unfortunately, and we spent a number of holidays youth hostelling in Scotland.

Holidays were also taken as a family, usually in a caravan at Talybont, near Harlech on the Welsh coast. Later, from the age of about twelve or thirteen, we found a cottage to rent in a village called Darowen, near Machynlleth. Darowen was a thriving community of approximately twenty cottages, (possibly fifty or sixty people) a school, infants and juniors and a church and a chapel. There was no pub or shop and Welsh was spoken almost exclusively, although most people spoke English too. Everyone was extremely friendly and we were always made very welcome. Our immediate neighbours were a family of six, three generations, who owned two slightly larger semi-detached cottages and invariably invited us to Sunday afternoon tea. This was a magnificent affair which included cold ham and other meats, salads, hot potatoes, desserts, cheese and homemade pickles. Afterwards, I always played a game of snooker with the grandfather, a very elderly, quietly spoken, Welshman.

The village was so isolated that our water supply (everyone's in the village) was from a pump on the green. Electricity had only arrived a few months before our first visit (1957) and the toilets entailed a trip across the lane that ran through the centre of the village, round to the back of the farmhouse that supplied us with milk straight from the cow, to a line of individual chemical loos. These were unlit of course, but I think each cottage had its own.

Darowen was where I gained my love of walking. It was surrounded by mountains, forests and rivers and I would go off for a day with a packed lunch and a map and compass and walk for miles.

From the age of eleven or twelve, I and various other friends would go camping for a week or so in August. Each year we moved a little further away from home in Shropshire. In 1960, when I was almost fifteen, four or five of us camped near a village called Glazley, some three or four miles south of Bridgenorth.

Most sets of parents would visit us at least once and on the occasion that my close friend Anthony's parents came, his father, having first condemned the campsite as being untidy – 'not as it would have been when I was a lad.' –, then told us they used to 'live off the land' when they camped. This seemed a good idea to us so the next day off we went in search of provisions.

We came across a market garden where we could make forays and take more or less anything that we wanted. We filled up a rucksack, which belonged to muggins (me), and proceeded back to the campsite. On the way, for reasons known only to young teenage boys, we lit a fire in the middle of the lane. No sooner had we done this than we heard a small motorbike approaching. We climbed a gate into a field and hid behind a hedge. The motorbike stopped on reaching the fire and David, being the tallest of our group, cautiously glanced over the hedge and ducking down quickly said, "It's a copper!" The policeman had obviously seen his head appear and ordered us out. He enquired as to why we had lit the fire and not receiving a satisfactory answer, because we couldn't think of one, asked what was in my bulging rucksack. I shamefacedly showed him the cornucopia of lettuces, radishes, tomatoes, marrows, potatoes and some fruit. He took possession of the lot and asked where we had taken it from and where we were camping; and then he told us to await his return.

We were terrified, youngsters had a healthy respect for the police in those days, so awaited his return with some trepidation. However, when he appeared with my empty rucksack, he said that the owner of the market garden did not intend to prosecute us as all his produce had been returned. With some relief, we offered him a cup of tea, which he accepted but turned down the offer of acorn and nettle soup complete with small floating maggots and said, with a wry smile, that his wife was expecting him home for steak and kidney pie.

We tried the soup but even with most of the maggot type creatures removed, our hearts weren't in it. All we could think of was steak and kidney pie. To complete a somewhat unsuccessful day of 'living off the land', we ate several pound of bullace (wild plums) that we had picked on the way back and spent a probably deserved night of stomach pains and diarrhoea.

On the whole, I thoroughly enjoyed my schooldays and was sorry to leave.

Chapter Five
Noddy

In my last year at school (1961), my closest friend was a lad called Christopher Norton, Noddy, a lad that I had known since junior school. We had been on a few walking and climbing holidays together in Wales and Shropshire. Having both left school in July of that year, we planned a week walking and climbing in the Lake District immediately after Christmas and the New Year of 1961/62.

We hitchhiked up to Kendal and as it wasn't late, although dusk, decided to carry on to the youth hostel at Bowness on Windermere, some nine or ten miles. Although it had started to snow, we reckoned that even if we didn't get a lift, which we didn't, it would only be a two and a half to three hour walk. Unfortunately, it started to snow more heavily which made the going much more difficult. After about five miles, whilst passing an isolated house, a man shouted to us asking where we were going. We replied Bowness, and then his wife appeared and invited us in for a hot drink and also made us some sandwiches. Her husband said we still had some five miles to go and that the road conditions were sure to be getting worse. I suppose that because they could see how young we were, they were concerned for our welfare and said we could stop the night there if we wished. However, being sixteen-year-olds, we thanked them for the offer and the tea and sandwiches and pressed on.

It was now about nine p.m. and snowing more and more, to the extent that it took us until midnight to walk the last five miles. I can't remember whether we called at the youth hostel and it was closed, or whether we didn't bother because it was so late; but seeing a police station, we went in and asked if they could suggest anywhere for the night. We were directed by the officer on duty to the local gas works, where, he said, that very often people put up for the night as it was warm and sheltered. We found our way there and explained that we had been sent from the police station and were shown up to a first floor area which was nice and warm and had three manhole covers set into the floor. We stretched out using our rucksacks and ropes as pillows, relieved to be finally out of the cold and fell asleep quickly. When I awoke in the morning and tried to wake Noddy, he was dead – overcome by fumes from one of the manholes.

As the coroner stated at the inquest, no one was really to blame, it was one of those tragic accidents.

If only we had not been foolhardy youngsters and had taken up the offer of the couple in the cottage to stay overnight; or if only we had arrived earlier and booked into the youth hostel. Perhaps we shouldn't have been sent there by the police or allowed to stay by the men working there; but it had been done before with no adverse consequences.

After the inquest and funeral, I visited Noddy's grave a few times before I left Wolverhampton for good, when I first moved to Shrewsbury and then to Nottingham. However, in January 2011, Gill and I went and found it again almost fifty years to the day of the funeral.

It was sad to reflect that I had already had fifty years of life longer than my friend.

Although it was never the same after Noddy's death, I did continue to climb and walk (mostly in Wales) with another friend, George, and a group of lads from Birmingham that we had met whilst climbing on Cader Idris.

On one of these breaks, I think in August 1962, camping near Machynlletth, I met a local girl, Nesta, in a coffee bar in the town. She was nice looking with blonde, wavy hair but appeared to be ostracised by the other girls that we had got to know – mainly, I think, because she had an English accent although she was Welsh. This was a lucky meeting in the sense that our normal venues were pubs: The Skinner's Arms in the town or The Red Lion at Dinas Mawddwy, if we were up that way.

Her parents had a farm near to 'Mach' and although her father detested me (for being English) we managed to keep our relationship, albeit a long distance one, going until not long before I moved to Nottingham.

Chapter Six

From the age of fifteen or sixteen, my ambition was focused in two different directions – either to go into The Forestry Commission or to own my own restaurant. I had stayed on at school until I was sixteen to take 'O levels' but from the age of fourteen had worked part time in a restaurant in Shropshire where I had gained my interest in cooking. The lady proprietor, Mrs Preston, was an Elizabeth David type, the daughter of some obscure Scottish earl (I believe). She had travelled extensively, especially in Italy, and at the age of sixty-three, had bought a large Georgian house between Wolverhampton and Bridgnorth and opened it as a rather nice, but sniffily snobbish, restaurant called The Thornescroft.

I was fascinated by the food, risottos, pastas, veal dishes, and others, all of course which have been 'old hat' for many years now but at that time 1959/60, were positively exotic to a working class boy and in fact to most people in Britain.

When I was sixteen, I did apply to join The Forestry Commission but eventually decided against it. The problem that I foresaw was trying to live on the two pounds a week bursary (I'm sure my memory serves me correctly) that one was paid whilst on the four-year training course. Two years of this were spent at university and the other two actually working in forests. You were not given the long vacations that students usually have, so no opportunity to earn extra money and my parents were not in a position to help financially. Because I was now earning seven pounds per week at the restaurant and eating food that very few sixteen-year-olds could dream of, I opted to stay in catering.

Mrs Preston, probably because of her antecedents, was an odd mixture of snobbery and a belief that the lower classes had certain rights. Probably a sense of 'noblesse oblige' I imagine! One of the ways that it manifested itself was in her deciding to open a tiny café in a room off the main kitchen, with its own entrance. Here, any passing local, walker or cyclist could come in and demand such delicacies as egg, chips and beans or breakfast at any time during the day. This very often presented huge problems for us chefs, as we may have been in the middle of producing a meal in the restaurant, consisting of, let's say, a lobster thermidor followed by a brace of partridge, only to have the bell ring in the café and beans on toast and pot of tea for two demanded! The head chef, Charles, remonstrated with Mrs Preston about this for the duration of time that I worked there, but to no avail.

Dinner in the restaurant was well beyond the means of the ordinary working person – probably about my weekly wage – for a couple. In those days the average skilled worker's wage was about £15 or £16 per week. My father, an electrical engineer, earned just about this figure, although he did have a car supplied with his job too. This incidentally, gave my mother the opportunity to 'queen it' over their friends and neighbours, as no one else owned a car at that time. This somewhat irritating trait in my mother created a bit of a rift between us when I was living in Nottingham. On one visit home –and although I was a conscientious son still paying my parents four pounds per week, even though I had not lived at home for two years – she asked me if I would mind arriving at night in future, so that the neighbours wouldn't see my long hair.

I became a 'conscientious objector' for some time after this!

Chapter Seven
Gill's Early days

Gill was born in 1947, in Eastbourne, where her parents owned a guesthouse. They had taken the lease on the property in 1946, moving from Blackpool to do so. She had three siblings – two sisters, fourteen and eleven years older – and a brother six years her senior.

Her mother was forty-four when she gave birth to Gill and so, probably because of her age, was very Victorian in outlook. One of her more eccentric ideas, when Gill was about seven or eight, was to plaster Gill's chest in goose grease – to keep out chills – and cover this with a large square of lint. During the school day, the grease would warm up and ooze through her blouse, much to the delight and amusement of her school friends.

Another source of acute embarrassment to Gill, was when her mother's dog, a cocker spaniel, came into 'season'. A local 'canine Casanova', a Labrador named Sandy, would lurk outside the guesthouse and on Gill's coming out to cycle to school, would chase after her down the seafront. He would then position himself in the playground, where he could keep an eye on her in the classroom and then repeat the performance on the way home.

Gill was brought up in a completely different environment to myself. There were quite a few Italians and Cypriots amongst the town's population, who had appeared after the War. In a sense, hers was quite a cosmopolitan upbringing, as many of her school friends were from these communities. She also had the beach and The Downs as a playground and by all accounts was a bit of a tomboy as a child. Eastbourne had a great many bomb sites until several years after the War. Many of these being large Victorian properties and guesthouses, still contained furnishings which provided intriguing places to explore for Gill and her friend, Andy, who lived in the same road. Others had no floors at all to speak of and the two of them would clamber about on rafters which were three or four storeys high. On one occasion, while clambering on some scaffolding, she slipped and was only saved by her skirt hem catching on a protruding pole. She hung there, somewhat inelegantly, for the best part of an hour while Andy went in search of an adult to rescue her.

Gill was strong-willed and frequently used to run off at the age of three or four, even though she knew that when she returned home, usually brought by the police, as she was on a number of occasions, she would receive a thrashing with a cane from her mother. When they went to the beach or the Western Lawns as a family, her parents would take a stake and a length of rope. The stake would be driven into the sand or grass and Gill attached to it by the rope around her waist; so enabling her parents to have a nap without fear of her absconding. Parenting was different in those days, although, as already mentioned, Gill's mother being the age she was, probably had something to do with it.

At the age of eight or so, she flatly refused to continue going to church, apparently the reason being that as she was not confirmed she was not allowed to partake of the wine! She has been an atheist ever since and quickly converted me when we met. However, she and her friend, Andy, were not above being bribed by a neighbour to occasionally attend Christian Science meetings, the going rate being two and sixpence each! Unfortunately, this came to another drastic end when her mother discovered what they were up to.

Gill attended a comprehensive school until she was fifteen and could have stayed on to take 'O levels' but chose instead to go on to secretarial college. Unfortunately, she became the black sheep of the family quite soon after starting college by becoming pregnant; so only completed some three months of the course. Her daughter, Karen, was born shortly after her sixteenth birthday. However, it must be said that after the initial shock, her parents did their very best to help her.

Chapter Eight
Parents

Both of my parents were born and brought up in Wolverhampton, although both families have been traced back by my sister to Clun (on the border of Wales) on my mother's side and Church Stretton in Shropshire, on my father's.

My father trained initially as a toolmaker and during the Second World War, worked at Bolton and Pauls, a factory producing aeroplanes, and also served as an air raid warden. Later he retrained as an electrician, which was his father's occupation. Prior to his apprenticeship as a toolmaker, he spent several months in Wales with his father who had a contract to install electricity in Llwyngwril, a coastal village.

Although having finished his education at fourteen years of age, as most children did then, he had a grasp of maths to a much higher level; which was a great help to me at school. He could quote from Shakespeare until his audience fell asleep and was the best exponent of *Albert and the Lion* that I have heard. He also played a number of musical instruments which gave him a popularity at parties, that wasn't quite as evident when he chose to quote Shakespeare! Dad was a strong person both physically and mentally but with a very easy-going nature, in short, the perfect father. From the age of about four or five he would take me to the football match at Molineux on Saturdays. Wolves were a premier team then with a number of internationals, including (as already mentioned), Billy Wright, England's captain, Bert Williams (goal), Ron Flowers and Jimmy Mullen. We kids were allowed to sit on the pitch in those days and see the likes of Stanley Matthews working his magic.

There was no such thing as crowd trouble, even though there were fifty to sixty thousand people all standing and all shouting their encouragement – or in the case of the referee, good natured abuse. If anyone fainted, they would be passed unceremoniously above the heads of the crowd down to the pitch, where, with a little fresh air, hopefully they would recover. It was all part of the Saturday afternoon entertainment.

My mother, as is very often the case, was temperamentally completely the opposite of my father. She was as volatile as he was calm. I often felt that on occasions, her fiery temper overcame her common sense. Later in life, I put this down to her Celtic roots (a wild and emotional race), but also apportioned part of the blame to King Offa for his lack of foresight in not constructing his border barrier (Offa's Dyke) to a sufficiently insurmountable height.

I jest of course, because in all other respects, she was the perfect mother. She was an excellent cook and besides bringing up three children, worked most of her life to help with the household income, to ensure a good standard of living for us all.

Together, they provided my brother, sister and myself with a very happy childhood.

As previously mentioned, Gill's parents moved to Eastbourne from Blackpool shortly after the War.

Her father was in the RAF and spent most of the War in Africa, where he managed to contract malaria, which revisited him on an annual basis for the rest of his life. He had a short career as goal keeper for Crystal Palace football club, whilst working at his normal trade as a bookbinder. He met Gill's mother, who was married and had a small bed and breakfast in Great Yarmouth, through his boss who was her brother-in-law.

Alice, Gill's mother, left her first husband and she and Harry (Gill's father) moved to Blackpool in 1938.

During the First World War, as a young girl, Alice was one of the first people ever to experience aerial bombing when a Zeppelin dropped a number of bombs on Great Yarmouth.

Chapter Nine
Summer 1965

These were wonderful days to be young and carefree. We held lots of parties between the house and the beach in Pevensey Bay. Wendy and Lyn, our friends from Nottingham, had moved down to Eastbourne; Bill and Wendy were now an item and so were Denton and Lyn. We were occasionally visited by the local policeman, PC Beoh, to be reprimanded for parties that were too noisy or that went on too late. He also wanted to keep check that the variety of cars that we now possessed were taxed and insured but on the whole, we had a pretty good relationship with him.

Although it was the 'swinging sixties' there was not really a drug culture, the only problems usually were with uninvited guests. We all drank but rarely to excess. Without doubt, the most important thing in our lives was sex, and I had found the sexiest girl in Eastbourne.

The music that we enjoyed was very much the popular songs of the sixties. The Beatles, Leonard Cohen, Bob Dylan, The Kinks and myriad others. A song that we claimed as our own was Sonny and Cher's *I've got you Babe*, closely followed by *Down Town* and *Funny How Love Can Be* by the Ivy League. The latter one reminding us of when we had had an argument and I seriously thought of returning to Nottingham.

We both liked folk music and Gill had a fairly extensive knowledge of classical music; which, over time, I started to learn more about and enjoy.

In September 1965, I was offered the job that I had been turned down for in May, at The Landsdowne Hotel, and so was now earning a regular salary. Gill was a wigmaker, which also paid very well. We bought a Mini Cooper S between us and could afford to eat out and have weekends away in reasonable hotels. From the beginning of our relationship, we had adopted a small Greek restaurant in Eastbourne, where although the food was at best average, we continued to use until the son of the original owner sold up in 2010.

Our favourite hotel for a weekend away, for many years, was The Unicorn in Stow-on-the-Wold. The first time we stayed there was in

April 1966, on our way up to Wolverhampton to visit my family. We arrived rather late, about nine p.m., so the restaurant was closed. However, a young assistant manager cooked gammon, egg and chips for us for the princely sum of one pound and eight pence (old money). Our bed and breakfast tariff was three pounds ten shillings for a double room. We loved The Unicorn and stayed there literally dozens of times over the years, including our honeymoon in 1968. We always asked for the same room (room 3) which was at the side of the building and overlooked the Fosse Way, as this was the room we had stayed in on our first visit. The food in the restaurant was usually of an excellent standard and after a good dinner we would move to the lounge, where there was always a roaring log fire, for coffee and brandies. Later we would adjourn to our room; making love late into the night and eventually drifting off to sleep to be woken with breakfast in bed the following morning. Our last visit was in 1993 on our twenty-fifth wedding anniversary, when the bill for four nights came to a fairly astonishing £600.

We stopped going to The Unicorn, not because of the cost but because the hotel and for that matter, the Cotswolds, were not as they used to be, both had become twee. Times change and of course, we had changed too.

An early trip that we made was to the Lake District and then onto Scotland. This was probably the first time that Gill was made aware of my passion for mountain walking. She was kitted out with boots, anorak and rucksack et cetera. Initially she was quite excited by the idea but having booked into a farm near Wastwater for bed and breakfast the first night, her excitement turned to alarm when I said, "We are going up there," pointing towards Scafell. We set off and climbed steadily for an hour or so, but looking back I saw she was sitting on a rock some fifty metres below. I went back down and found her in tears, complaining bitterly that she didn't like boots or mountains and that she had never had a boyfriend like me before and sincerely hoped, that once having got rid of me, she would not have the misfortune to meet anyone similar!

After a little cajoling, I got her moving again by telling her that there was a café higher up, knowing that Gill's second most pleasurable pastime was eating. Fortunately the mist came down and we descended, which avoided the looming argument had we reached the top and for Gill to discover that no café existed.

Eventually she became, and still is, a strong walker.

The Monster

When we reached Scotland, after staying with some friends based in Drymen, we drove up to Loch Lomond and pitched our tent for the night on the eastern shore, three or four miles south of Rowardennan. We were cooking a meal while it was still light, although dusk was on its way, when we heard a splashing in the water some ten yards away. There in the loch (and I expect no one to believe this), gliding past no more than twenty-five to thirty yards away, was a smaller version of the definitive Loch Ness Monster. Its head (which was small) and neck stood some five feet above the surface and was followed by a wake. A number of seagulls were flying round it. It turned and went past in the opposite direction and then turned again and appeared to be coming closer to the shoreline. I don't think many things made me nervous when I was that age but we didn't hang around to see how close it was coming. We jumped in the car and headed towards Rowardennan, stopping at a pub we had seen earlier. We had a drink and related the tale to the merriment of the locals, whose consensus was that it was either a 'highland beastie' or we had been drinking prior to our arrival! Neither was the case.

We ate in the pub as we had left our meal and table and chairs in situ and as there was no way we were going back until morning, we slept in the car overnight. When we returned in daylight, everything was as we had left it with the exception that our meal had disappeared, all that remained was a couple of well licked billycans. We assumed that a passing fox was probably the most likely culprit as tinned burgers seemed unlikely fare for a monster!

Another holiday at this time was a week's tour of Wales and the Lake District, starting in the Cotswolds. This was November/December 1966.

We had arranged to go with Lyn and Denton but unfortunately Lyn could not get the time off work, so the three of us set off, staying at The Unicorn the first night and at The Skinner's Arms in Machynlleth, one of my old abodes when climbing, the second. The third night was spent at the Prince Llewellyn in Beddgelert, where Gill and I had a room overlooking the river. We then drove straight up to the Lake District staying overnight in Kendal. The following morning we headed north through Windermere and Keswick and then round and over the Honister Pass. It was snowing quite heavily here and the only other person we saw was a man equipped with a shovel and broom, who appeared to be single-handedly attempting to clear the pass. We stopped and chatted to him for a while and he told us that when he had cleared Honister, he was going over to the Hardknott Pass to clear that too! We assumed that he was joking but were not quite sure.

We stayed at the Grange Hotel on the side of Loweswater for a couple of nights for the princely sum of six pounds six shillings, including one dinner. The next day we drove south through Egremont and then along Eskdale to try the Hardknott Pass. Just prior to the pass we came across an inn called Tatigarth and as it was lunchtime, stopped for a drink and something to eat. The inn was owned and run by a hippyish couple from London, Mike and Sybil. As there was no one else there we chatted to them at some length and then Mike took us out to a rear room to show us some damson wine that he had made. This potent mixture was contained in a large bath. We sampled some of it and as it wasn't bad we took several jugs back into the bar, where there was a roaring log fire. The afternoon drifted on and everything took on a 'rosy hue'; the company, the music (Leonard Cohen) and the venue becoming more and more convivial, we decided to stop for the night. I remember at some stage going outside to see a donkey which Mike then rode round his field, but as he was facing the donkey's tail, he of course fell off. We had to carry him comatose back in to the bar. There was also a vague recollection of eating steak and chips, but at what time, I have no idea. Breakfast was a much more subdued affair but with the wonderful recovery rate of youth, we all felt much better after it.

Sybil had mentioned that a friend of hers ran a pub called The George at Hubberholme in the Yorkshire dales. As this was more or less our intended route, we asked if she would telephone and reserve us a couple of rooms for that night. We set off with a couple of bottles of Mike's damson wine and headed over Hardknott Pass. The Pass had been cleared sufficiently to be able to get through, whether or not by our friend from Honister we don't know! We arrived at The George about seven p.m., having missed our way once in the dark. Gill caused a bit of a sensation with the locals by standing in front of the fire in her mini skirt and thigh length boots.

For the three of us, including a good meal of ham and eggs, drinks, coffee and bed and breakfast, the total bill was six pounds three shillings.

I mention a lot of these costs for both the interest of prices then but also because at the time of writing, Gill recently paid fifteen shillings (seventy-five pence) for one tomato!

The following night we stayed further down the valley at an inn called The Hare and Hounds. The landlord here was Jacko, a very friendly and hospitable host. After a very good dinner of steak and kidney pie, we sat around a roaring log fire in a massive inglenook with some locals, one of whom was playing a guitar. Jacko appeared with an accordion and we had a most enjoyable and memorable evening singing folk songs.

It is sad to think that this type of inn has long disappeared. Although the buildings are the same, the plain but good food and spontaneous hospitality have gone, replaced in many cases, although not all, by affected landlords and untrained chefs trying to imitate their betters, but lacking the skill or flair to do so.

UNICORN HOTEL
STOW-on-the-WOLD 135
GLOUCESTERSHIRE.
Telephone - Stow-on-the-Wold 257

Room No. 3 .... (?April) 1964

Mr. Castor

	£	s	d
Bed and Breakfast	3	10	.
Lunch			
Dinner	1	<	8
Bar		2.	.
Extras			
A.N. Tea			
Room Service		2	<
	4	14	8
10%		9	6
£	5	4	2

UNICORN HOTEL
STOW-on-the-WOLD
GLOUCESTERSHIRE
Telephone : Stow-on-the-Wold 257 65

Room No. 15/18 .... 26/11/196?

Mr. Castor

	£	s	d
Bed and Breakfast	5	12	6
Lunch			
Afternoon Tea			
Dinner			
Supper			
Dining Room Drinks			
Bar Rm Service		6	.
Coffee			
Morning Tea		6	<
Newspapers		1	6
	6	6	.
Service Charge 10%		12	6
£	6	18	6

Telephone:
LAMPLUGH 211

THE GRANGE HOTEL,
LOWESWATER,
COCKERMOUTH Cumb.

2 | 12 19 66

Mr. & Mrs. CORDER — Room 6

To Mrs. E. J. NORMAN Dr.

	Full Board			
2	Bed and Breakfast	@ 23/6	2	7 0
2	Dinner, Bed and Breakfast	@ 29/6	3	11 0
	Dinners			
	Luncheons			
2	Afternoon Teas	@ 1/3	2	6
	Morning and Evening Teas 1/-	@ 2/6		
	1 Coffee + Sandwiches		3	6
	Wines, etc. 1 Lager		2	0
	Garage			
		£	6	6 0

THE GEORGE INN
HUBBERHOLME
via Skipton

4/12/66

3 bed + breakfast @ 27/6   £4 - 2 - 6

3 Hm ranges   £1 - 0 - 3
        4/9

3 Coffee 1/-   3 - 0
3 Tea 1/-   3 - 0

Drinks   4-6
         9-10   14 - 4

£ 6 - 3 · 1

1967

In about March of 1967, I was offered a position as chef at The Clifford Club, a new casino that had just opened in Eastbourne. The salary was twenty-five pounds per week for only five nights, the hours being seven thirty pm to eleven thirty pm. As this was only a couple of pounds less than I was earning at the hotel where I worked some fifty hours a week, it seemed, in modern parlance, a 'no brainer'. There were a number of other reasons why this would be a good move, not least because I had built up some quite substantial debts. I had a penchant for fashionable clothes and owned too many made to measure suits and sea island cotton shirts and apart from our going out quite a lot, there was also the expense of my flat and the loan on our car. The benefits would be twofold. Working five nights per week meant that we would be unable to go out to the extent we were doing and being free during the day would enable me to find other employment too. I found two extra jobs in small hotels, one for five days a week cooking breakfast and lunches and preparing the 'mis en place' for dinner and the other all day Sunday preparing their three meals. I found myself working about seventy plus hours per week, but the debts melted away very quickly.

A further reason for taking the job at the casino was that it was almost certainly only to be short term, just for the summer.

Chapter Ten
London

During the winter of 1966/67, many of our friends had left Eastbourne, the majority moving to London. I had decided that I wanted to take a hotel management course and so early in 1967, had applied for a position with Strand Hotels, a subsidiary of The Lyons Group. The salary was a pittance (seventeen pounds per week) but their training course had a good reputation and would, hopefully, eventually lead to a much better lifestyle for us. After an interview in London, I was offered a place on their course commencing in September 1967.

Gill and I knew that we wanted to spend our lives together and lingered for hours over meals or in bed after making love, talking of our hopes and aspirations. I knew that in Gill I had a girl who would always be a full partner in whatever we decided to do.

We had asked Gill's parents whether they would be willing to look after Karen, Gill's little daughter, for the two year period of my training course, to enable Gill to move with me. They were more than happy to do this and Gill would return to Eastbourne every weekend anyway. It wasn't an ideal situation but I saw little chance of improving our prospects by staying in Eastbourne. Once I had finished the course there would be lots of openings for us, probably as assistant managers initially, with a group such as Trusthouse Forte. Accommodation invariably came with these positions and then we would be able to have Karen with us. Later in the summer, Gill applied for, and was given, a job with Wig Specialities, a firm that did a lot of film work, at almost double my salary.

We rented a flat in Gypsy Hill, which was about an hour's journey to central London and as we were working completely different hours, Gill normal office hours and myself split shifts, we saw very little of each other. My main base was The Regent Palace Hotel in Piccadilly Circus, although I might have to be on duty at The Strand Palace and more regularly, The Cumberland at Marble Arch. At weekends, Gill would go down to Eastbourne by train to see Karen and work late on a Saturday night to complete another wig to earn extra money. If I had a Sunday off, I would drive down early in the morning after having stayed the night at The Regent Palace. This was the one time that I liked London, early on a Sunday morning driving from Piccadilly down through south London and out into the countryside with no one else about.

There was always a dinner and dance at the hotel on a Saturday night, much frequented by the London Jewish community. It was extremely good value at a guinea per head, which included a four course dinner and two big bands.

We always enjoyed our Sundays as it was the only time we really managed to spend together, perhaps having a pub lunch or taking Karen to the beach. In the evening, prior to our return to London, we would visit a couple of friends, Richard and Jill, and leave there about eleven pm for the drive back to town. On the way back we always stopped at an all-night kiosk type place at Thornton Heath for a coffee and a fairly disgusting sausage sandwich.

I didn't particularly enjoy living in London myself, I found it too big and impersonal but we saw it as a means to an end. However, on the rare occasions that I wasn't working, we had quite a good social life as most of our friends were there now. Our entertainment was usually in pubs and parties and the occasional visit to The Blue Boar in Leicester Square, a restaurant where the steaks were cooked in view – a new innovation then – but because of the lack of decent extraction/ventilation we were very often almost smoked out. We could not afford to go to the theatre but on one memorable occasion, we went to see Topol in *Fiddler on the Roof.* This rare treat was paid for by a well-known author whose daughter Denton was now seeing, having split up with Lyn.

During that summer in London, we managed to take a couple of breaks. Philip and Deane had invited us up to Nottingham, where they now lived, for the weekend, so one lovely Friday evening in early June, we set off up the M1. At some point north of Luton, Gill said that she could see the blue line of the Cotswolds over in the west. The attraction was too great and being young and thoughtless, we decided we would rather spend the weekend there.

Our intention, as always, was to head for Stow and The Unicorn, but as time was getting on, we stayed the first night in Brackley at the Crown Hotel. The following morning we drove to Oxford and then on to Stow. After spending the Saturday night at our favourite hotel, where we were quite well known by now and so were always looked after, we drove down to Stonehenge fairly early on the Sunday. In those days one could just wander around the Henge, which we did for a couple of hours, seeing no one else at all. We had a great weekend but Phil and Deane were, understandably, very annoyed with us.

Later that summer, having apologised to our friends and having been forgiven, we arranged a camping holiday with them. We borrowed a large, two bed tent from some friends of my parents and all met up one Saturday morning in Stow-on-the-Wold.

After a few drinks at lunchtime, we proceeded to the farmer's field that I had found. We had reserved a table for dinner back at The Unicorn and so put all the camping gear into Philip's car and returned to Stow in ours, giving no thought whatsoever of the likelihood of our being able to erect the enormous tent at all – let alone in the dark! On our return, we discovered that there were no instructions included, although they probably wouldn't have been much use anyway in our slightly inebriated state. After about an hour, all that we had achieved was a covered area about six feet square and some twenty-four inches in height. The girls became irritable and obnoxious and decided to sleep in one of the cars, whilst Philip and I, in a fit of obstinacy, crawled into our bivouac. Philip spent the night being sick, much to the amusement of Gill and Deane.

A strange occurrence that night – one which we all bore witness to – emanated from a small, derelict 'summer house', which stood on a grassy knoll some three hundred yards further up the small valley where we were camped. There were no other buildings within three quarters of a mile.

During the afternoon, prior to returning to Stow for dinner, we had looked over this small, round building which was completely empty and devoid of any glass in the windows, although the walls and roof were sound. Sometime in the early morning, probably about two or three o'clock, we were all woken by the sound of revelry coming from the summer house, but there were no lights showing at all. The following morning we investigated it again and found it to be exactly as the previous day.

In daylight, we managed to erect the tent after a fashion, although it never achieved the graceful lines one felt that it ought, and then went down into Naunton (the nearest village) for a Sunday lunchtime drink. One of the locals in there happened to be the farmer whose land we were camping on. We mentioned the revelry in the summer house and his reply was, "Oh! That was just the old people," and expanded no further.

The pub, The Black Horse, proved to be a good find, so we 'haunted it' for the rest of our stay.

Autumn 1968

Gill's parents had been trying to sell their guesthouse in Eastbourne for several years without success. Originally they had been asking £4,000 for the lease and goodwill, but had now dropped the asking price to £2,500. We had in fact approached a broker ourselves a couple of years earlier to see whether there was any possibility of raising funds. However, the answer had been an emphatic no and we were also told that it was hugely overvalued as there were only three years (at that time) left on the lease. Now though, we had managed to save £750 (no mean feat considering my salary). Gill's parents, probably in desperation, said that if we were still interested in buying the guesthouse and paid £500 as a deposit, we could pay off the residue over a four-year period at a set interest rate. We had to make a decision, as my training course would be coming to an end the following year and we would probably be looking to leave London. Weighing up the pros and cons, we knew that it was still overpriced as there was now effectively one trading season (1969) remaining before the end of the lease: but if we could be guaranteed an extension of the lease prior to purchase, then it would be a first step on the ladder of self-employment which is really what we both wanted.

I had long ago come to the conclusion that I would be much better off working for myself as I did tend to question orders from superiors, especially if I disagreed with them. This trait in me had been evident in my early teens.

When I was sixteen, I had gone along to an army recruiting office in Wolverhampton with a view to joining the 'junior leaders' – I think that was the title. Because I loved the outdoors, army life seemed very appealing, all that travel, camping, rock climbing, canoeing et cetera. However, on informing my mother that I might join up, she pointed out that it was most unlikely that I would see much of the great outdoors, as I was more likely to spend most of my time indoors, in 'clink' for insubordination.

We decided to go ahead with the purchase of the guesthouse and having negotiated a new, fourteen-year lease with the landlord, then signed the contracts with Gill's parents in early September, ready to take over the business in January 1969.

We both continued with our respective jobs until just before Christmas; and in the meantime decided to get married, which we did on October 5th 1968. The reception was held at The Landsdowne Hotel in Eastbourne (the hotel where I had worked) which allowed the ever-growing diaspora of our friends to attend from various parts of the country.

December 1968

Since deciding to move back to Eastbourne, we had been looking for a puppy for Karen, but it appeared that so had the rest of the population, as there were none to be had. Even Battersea Dogs' Home was empty but on enquiring there we were given the telephone number of someone in Oxted who wanted to get rid of their 'mutt'. I telephoned and then went to pick him up. He was a 'Heinz 57' about three months old. Disconcertingly, along with his collar, lead and dog bowl and food, I was given five pounds to take him away!

On the way back to Gypsy Hill he was sick, but quite impressively managed to vomit into our friend Bill's John Lennon cap that had been left on the rear seat.

The next day, the 19th December 1968, we moved back to Eastbourne to start a new chapter of our lives together.

Chapter Eleven
Eastbourne
Winter/Spring 1969

During the three or four months before we opened for our first season, it rapidly became apparent what we had taken on. The property needed a new roof, rewiring and complete refurbishment. The boiler, for hot water, was a solid fuel monstrosity which either had to be kept alight overnight, or if it went out, one had to rise at about five a.m. to relight it with sticks and rolled-up newspapers. Being young and not prone to getting up too early, most of the time I tried to keep it going all night, but eventually succeeded in burning a hole in the front casing.

There were fourteen bedrooms to accommodate twenty-eight guests, but only three toilets and one bathroom. Our loo downstairs was outside and there was a bath in the scullery where the washing up was also done – by hand! It seems incredible now in these days of en suite bathrooms, that people were prepared to queue for the loo and probably did not have a bath for a week – but they were and didn't. It felt to me as if I had regressed ten or fifteen years, as although I had never lived in a house with an outside toilet, I had known friends at school who had done.

Of course, none of the above works could be carried out as we had no savings left after paying the £500 deposit, solicitor's charges and other costs.

At Easter we opened and from there until the following winter, things were a little easier, although at a tariff rate of seven to eight guineas per person for full board, we were never going to make a fortune. Bengy (the dog) now renamed Morphine – we had had him since he was a 'poppy' – quickly made us aware why his previous owners had given me five pounds to take him away. He ate everything in sight, furniture, curtains, Karen's toys, plaster off the wall and even on one occasion two steaks that we had saved up for.

The next two or three years were particularly difficult, always trying to squeeze enough profit to keep up with the necessary repairs. Denton, who was a very good handyman, had split up with Lyn and moved back to Eastbourne to work for the 'bloke' who operated the speedboat off the pier. As he had no work in winter, he helped me with decorating for his board and lodging and I'm afraid, a pittance of pay. We were living meagrely and somewhat precariously on about five pounds per week, which had to include Denton too. Many of our meals were breast of lamb at sixpence each; these were turned into lamb stew, Friar Tuck's pudding, lamb pie and a roast which had been boned, rolled and stuffed – and probably other dishes that I have forgotten. Our only source of income during the winter months (October to April) was the deposits for the summer bookings. Our finances were helped after the first couple of years by letting out some of the bedrooms during the winter period to (mainly) Spanish waiters, usually working at The Grand Hotel. However, this wasn't especially viable (at two pounds a week) as the rooms needed, at the very least, a coat of paint prior to opening for the summer season.

In the winter of 1970/71, we had to have the roof renewed as water poured through sections of it every time it rained. It was suggested by the firm carrying out the work that we should have the old cast iron guttering replaced at the same time, i.e., while the scaffolding was in situ. The cost of doing this was an extra £200, which may as well have been £2000 for all the chance we had of raising it; so we said that it couldn't be done. They very often started work on the roof before we were up in the morning, as we had convinced ourselves that it was cheaper to stay in bed late – less food consumed, less heating, but more hanky-panky. One morning we heard a tremendous crashing of something being thrown down outside and on my looking out of the window, I saw that the workmen were tearing down the old guttering. I waited until they had finished and then telephoned the company to explain what had happened. There was a long pause from the manager and then in a resigned tone he said, "Well, I suppose we will have to renew it for you at no charge."

It was becoming increasingly obvious to us that we could not make sufficient profit in the short term to carry out all the necessary work. There was still the rewiring to do, a new gas boiler and an extra bathroom to install; and general refurbishment. Even more expensively, looming on the horizon, was the new Fire Precautions Act in regard to hotels and guesthouses. This would entail a lot of work such as installing a fire alarm system complete with smoke detectors in each room, building fireproof partitions and doors at each floor level and all bedroom doors to be brought up to half hour fire protection.

I was still keen on the idea of a restaurant and if we could buy or open one that traded all year, the cash flow would help with our immediate expenses. In the past we had discussed the possibility of a partnership in such a venture with our friend Bill. Bill had recently been to see us and had brought along his new girlfriend, Eve, a lovely Scottish girl from Edinburgh. We talked further about opening a restaurant together and as they both liked the idea of moving down to Eastbourne, we decided to start looking around.

Spring/Summer 1972

Bill and Eve moved to Eastbourne in early summer 1972, staying with us and living in the attic! Gill was now pregnant with our son, Rupert, and so Eve helped us in the guesthouse. Karen, our daughter, was now nine years of age and excited at the prospect of a little brother or sister.

We had seen a place for sale at £5,500. It was a complete dump, in a lock-up in Seaside, which could be described, at best, as a secondary trading position. The 'cuisine', cooked and served by the owner, a bloke in a dirty white T-shirt, who also owned two mangy dogs that hung around under the tables, was – and I use the term cautiously – Spanish. When he ducked under his bar flap, which for some reason was fixed, he exposed a builder's percentage of his backside for the delectation of his customers.

His version of paella was pudding rice cooked in packeted fish stock, with frozen prawns and chopped peppers thrown in. An alternative, mouth-watering, dish was 'biftec con Jerez'. This was a slice of Argentinian striploin with a concasse of mushrooms, peppers and tomatoes on top; the whole doused in cheap sherry, but for a special occasion a spot of brandy was added and then set alight at the table! You get the picture.

However, due more to his opening hours – midday until three a.m. – but also presumably the lack of sophistication of the eating out public of Eastbourne at that time, his turnover was some £300 per week.

With the optimism of youth, although without any real expectation, I made an appointment to see our bank manager, Dowson Brown, who hitherto I had never met, and put the proposition to him. He asked what percentage of the purchase price we would be able to contribute ourselves, but when I said, "Nothing," he chuckled and said that he couldn't entertain it. He then, out of politeness, asked how the guesthouse was going and what had I done before we had bought it? I told him about my training as a chef and my subsequent course in hotel management. He asked where I had worked as a chef and amongst others I mentioned The Chateau in Nottingham. He looked up from doodling on a pad and for the first time showed some interest. He asked when I had worked there and what position I had held. On my answering both questions, he then explained that he had moved some years ago from managing the main branch in Nottingham to Eastbourne, but whilst he was there and prior to Berni Inns taking over the restaurant, he had managed The Chateau's account. He said that as their bank manager, he had dined there frequently and therefore knew the standard of the restaurant and, of course, how successful it was. To my amazement, he then said he would agree the loan to purchase in full and would also allow us an overdraft of £250 to get us started. Over the succeeding years, we became good friends until long after his retirement. He was also a regular and valued customer in the restaurant.

Chapter Twelve
Fagins
September 1972-October 1973

On September 7th, after having served breakfast in the guesthouse, Gill went into hospital and our son, Rupert was born early the following morning. The day after, I told her we had bought a restaurant.

We decided to rename the restaurant Fagins as the London show, *Oliver*, was very popular at that time. I don't think it occurred to us that it may have been impolite, as the freehold of the premises (our landlords) was owned by the local synagogue, which in actual fact was situated over the restaurant. However, they didn't seem to mind.

The renamed restaurant eventually became very successful. However, initially on changing the menu over from pseudo-Spanish to bistro style food and steaks, we saw the turnover plummet by half. But within a month, with some advertising and promotions, we soon brought the takings back up and in fact increased them substantially. This was no mean feat, as we only opened six nights per week, seven p.m. until one a.m. Friday and Saturday and seven p.m. to eleven p.m. other nights. It was very hard work as I was the sole chef and although the restaurant only sat thirty covers, every Friday and Saturday we would turn over in excess of a hundred meals each night. We were lucky in one respect insomuch that there was very little competition in town. There was a good steak bar and a couple of good restaurants out in the country, one being The Hungry Monk (where Banoffi Pie was first created), but both being fairly expensive. At Fagins, people could eat good French provincial cooking at ninety-five pence per main course with homemade French onion soup and other first courses at eight pence to thirty pence. The most expensive dish on the menu was a T-bone steak (sixteen ounces in weight) which along with fries, tomatoes, mushrooms and salad, cost the princely sum of one pound twenty-five pence. It doesn't seem possible now.

Because we were one of the few restaurants open on a Sunday evening, we had quite a procession of people who were appearing at The Congress Theatre. Among others, Steeleye Span, Nigel Davenport and David Jason (who turned up covered in oil, as their car had broken down) and Tommy Cooper who became a regular as he had a cottage in Eastbourne. Tommy was a huge man and always wore the same long, mac-type overcoat, which had the effect of making him look even bigger still. His head was equally large and he would always poke it through the hatch into the kitchen to say good evening to me. Pandemonium usually reigned when he came in, he was very popular and would usually tour the restaurant cracking jokes and generally 'acting the goat'. He and his wife always ordered steaks and occasionally asked us to wrap them for them to take away. We would order them a taxi and more than once found a steak on the pavement outside where it had dropped out of the pocket of his gigantic overcoat!

In March of 1973, we bought the lease on an empty shop and shopfitted it ourselves as a takeaway fried chicken/ ribs et cetera unit and called it The Kentucky Inn. This was a new innovation for Eastbourne as the nearest fried chicken outlet was in Brighton. On our opening night (in June) we had in excess of a hundred people queuing for takeaways.

There was plenty of accommodation above The Kentucky, which proved to be very useful as the guesthouse was becoming decidedly cramped.

We had managed to raise some extra funds from the bank in order to build an extension at the rear of Elmscroft. This was to be a bedroom for us along with an en suite shower and toilet. It was due to be ready by April 1973 but unfortunately the builders that we had employed proved to be less than useless, which meant that there was no chance of it being ready for the summer season. When we reopened the guesthouse in April, Bill and Eve – and their son who was born in January 1973 – had to move back into the attic. Gill and I slept on a mattress on the kitchen floor, Karen was on a Z-bed in the dining room and Rupert slept in a drawer.

By about mid-June, we had managed to sort out the accommodation above The Kentucky, sufficiently for Bill, Eve and their son, Bobby, to move in. There were a number of other spare rooms, so my sister, Marylyn, who had moved down to Eastbourne and was working part time at Fagins, took one of them and the 'Pest' – an aspiring DJ who worked in both restaurants in any capacity, took another.

The Pest was regularly arrested for minor misdemeanours, which was always very inconvenient if he was supposed to be working – which he always was. One of his less bright ideas was to hire a car and not return it on the due date. At about ten p.m. on a Saturday night, round came a sergeant who we had got to know quite well and declared in his strong Welsh accent, that he had come to arrest the 'boyo' (the Pest) for non-return of a hire vehicle. I pleaded with him to allow the 'Pest' his freedom until the end of the session (about two a.m.) as we were so busy and couldn't manage without him. The sergeant agreed to this and said he would return later, which he duly did. I somehow can't imagine that happening now! The Pest was incarcerated over the weekend and I had to go and bail him out on Monday morning.

We left the Pest one night to clean the carpets in Fagins, after closing. On receiving my telephone bill sometime later, there was a huge sum relating to a number of telephone calls to Memphis, USA. On enquiring of the Pest as to the reason for these calls, he said that he had been offered a one-night gig in a club in Eastbourne and had been trying to find out how much it would cost to get Elvis over for the venue! He was quite serious and pointed out, with some indignation, that he had asked for the call charges to be reversed. I think he washed up for a whole week without pay, to recompense us.

When one is young (I was twenty-seven at the time) one can do a phenomenal amount of work. However, as the summer wore on, finishing cooking for a hundred people at Fagins and not getting to bed until three or four a.m. and then having to be up at six a.m. for breakfast at the guesthouse, inevitably the strain began to tell.

During the day, Gill and me would be cooking huge pots of coq au vin/carbonnade of beef/estouffade and many other dishes for Fagins; and portioning dozens of chickens and spare ribs for The Kentucky. Besides which, breakfast and dinner for twenty-eight people had to be prepared in the guesthouse, along with Gill having two children to look after too.

Fagins was starting to become a bit of a love/hate relationship. We enjoyed Sunday nights when Gill and I, with the Pest washing up, worked on our own and about once a month on a Sunday lunchtime, we went to a wine tasting at Druscilla's, who supplied our Spanish house wine. Karen, our daughter, being a little older, was left with grandparents and Rupert in his carrycot, was usually left beside a huge Stilton on the wine tasting table.

Although we never had any real trouble in the restaurant as we had a barman/bouncer, Big Jim, and very often the sergeant or other police officers that we knew were having coffee in the kitchen. We occasionally had irritating customers. People who had had too much to drink prior to coming in and might profess that there was no wine in the coq au vin or beer in the carbonnade for example.

Occasionally, things would blow up, usually because of something trivial. One busy Saturday night, Gill took an order for a steak on which the customer had requested no salad. In a rush, the meal went out with its usual salad garnish and a few seconds later, Gill appeared in the kitchen and scraped it off. In my usual 'pleasant and calm' manner, I shouted at her to get out of my way, which she did, but then hurled the whole meal back at me through the hatch! She then stormed out and walked home, too angry to take notice of the stares and ribald comments as she stamped through the centre of town in her Fagins' uniform of a mob-cap and Nell Gwynne type, low cut dress. Meanwhile, in my fury, I had gone into the restaurant and ordered everyone out; enlightening them with the perfectly logical explanation for this proposed exodus that I'd had enough and was going for a drink! There was deathly silence but no one moved, in fact no one moved at all. Most people seemed to be frozen in time, with a glass of wine or a fork full of food halfway between plate and mouth; but all looking in my direction.

Bill, Jim and the Pest, physically dragged me back into the kitchen and after a few minutes I calmed down and carried on.

An interesting sequel to this incident was that, although as previously mentioned, we could only seat about thirty people at any one time, over the next few years several hundred mentioned that they had been dining at Fagins that night.

We had a few memorable customers, some because of their eccentricity and others just because they were nice people. One that I got to know quite well was a giant steel erector who was working in the town. On the first night that we took over, Jack, the previous owner, was supposed to have come in to help me wade through the mysteries of the 'Spanish cuisine'. Needless to say, he didn't turn up. I was completely 'up the wall' trying to replicate his disgusting dishes and at the same time, trying to stop Bill from doing anything other than garnishing the plates, when a T-bone that I was cooking went up in flames. I yanked it off the grill and threw it in the sink, where the Pest put it out with a fire extinguisher. Having then realised it was the last T-bone we had, I washed it off, put it on the grill again and sent it in. Half an hour later a waitress came back with a clean plate and said that the customer (the steel erector) had said it was the worst steak that he had ever eaten and when was Jack coming back? As it had quietened down now, I went out and apologised, leaving out any mention of the fire extinguisher, and said there would be no charge. Noting the size of him, I also offered to cook him a twelve ounce sirloin if he felt he could manage it, to which he said that he could. From that time on, each Friday or Saturday when he came in, he would have a sirloin as first course followed by a T-bone as a main, both with all the accompaniments.

We had a number of other odd/eccentric regular customers, notably the 'Gay Gourmet', a bloke of about fifty who dressed flamboyantly and acted like Oscar Wilde; and who always came in with new 'pretty' young men. The 'Donkey Man', a well-dressed rep, who lived a few doors down from Fagins and for some inexplicable reason (we never found out why) stabled a donkey in his small garden at the rear and in view of our kitchen.

Another group were some friends of Big Jim, the barman, all motorbike lads who would roar up at about midnight on a Friday straight from the King's Nightclub, eat a T-bone and then return to the club until it closed. Not to be forgotten, although not a paying customer, was Fritz the Cat, who had appeared the day we took over and had adopted us as an upmarket meal ticket. Fritz (an all-black cat) was well known to the regular customers and provided endless amusement especially on really busy nights. Having been thrown out of the back door of the kitchen, he would race along the passageway into Susans Road and wait outside the entrance to the restaurant until the next customers came in. He would then tear down the centre aisle of the restaurant heading for the kitchen again, urged on by shouts of encouragement from the diners, only to be thrown out of the back door yet again. A dozen times a night was not unusual.

My relationship with Bill, unfortunately, continued to deteriorate and although I am sure I was not blameless in this, the main problem was that he could not be bothered with the minutiae of running a business. I am, of course, certain that he would not agree with that assessment.

The only time that I can remember agreeing with Bill over anything, was in our decision to sell the restaurants and end the partnership. Gill and I had already discussed it at some length and although the two businesses were very successful, we had decided we would be better off selling them and reverting to being on our own.

The Kentucky was sold in August and Fagins went in October of 1973.

We eventually managed to complete the extension at the rear of Elmscroft and along with the extra money earned from Fagins and The Kentucky, life became a little easier.

Bill and Eve moved back to Liverpool and although it was a pity because I liked Bill personally and Eve was very easy-going, life was definitely calmer without him. He and Eve eventually split up and Bill has since remarried.

Gill and I plodded on at Elmscroft for a further two years, having placed it permanently 'on the market'.

Karen was quite a help with her little brother who became a bit of a scamp. He managed to create havoc in the dining room on a couple of occasions. Once by replacing the sugar in a number of sugar bowls with salt and an even more memorable morning, had managed to put dried spaghetti into some of the teapots. Our attention was drawn to this by screams from the dining room, as guests poured tea and watched in horror as what looked like long, white worms wriggled out of the spouts into their cups!

HAVE YOU TRIED?

FAGIN'S

BISTRO AND STEAK HOUSE

26a SUSANS ROAD

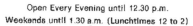

Open Every Evening until 12.30 p.m.
Weekends until 1.30 a.m. (Lunchtimes 12 to 2)

OUR EXTENSIVE MENU INCLUDES

Giant "T" Bone Steak	£1.25
(One pound uncooked weight)	
Sirloin, 12 to 14 oz.	£1.05
Half a succulent Chicken	90p
Mouth watering Half Duckling	£1.05
Coq-au-Vin	90p
Beef Bourguignonne	95p
Biff Medloc	90p
Pork Tropicana	85p
Steak Pipranata	98p

All the above dishes served complete with vegetables. No Cover Charge. No Service Charge.

During November couples arriving before 10 p.m. Monday to Thursday will receive a FREE Half Caraf of Wine.

Bookings — 21263 or 26588

Chapter Thirteen
Winter 1974/74

I went along to a Hotels Association meeting early in September. The meeting had been arranged by a travel company (SAGA) who we and several other hotels and guesthouses dealt with. Their modus operandi then – although they are a much bigger company now – was to bring holidaymakers to a resort by chartered train and place them into accommodation that they had contracted during the 'shoulder months' of a season, i.e. April/May and September/October. Their rates were quite low, some nine pounds a week for full board, but there was little other business about in those days during these months. The Eastbourne hoteliers who had contracts with the company never did anything but complain about the tariff rates, so Sidney de Haan (the chairman) and his son, Roger (the MD) had decided to come to Eastbourne to try to explain their position.

The meeting started good-naturedly with Roger pointing out that rates could not be increased in Eastbourne without other resorts wanting the same; and that in any case they were in competition with coach operators and therefore had to keep a competitive price. When it became obvious the company wasn't going to be moved, the meeting deteriorated into a baying mob who were unwilling to listen further. As the chairman of the meeting, an Eastbourne hotelier, appeared to have lost the plot, I stood up and asked if I could speak. I pointed out that no one was forced into a contract with SAGA and that surely anyone that felt they could drum up sufficient business during these shoulder months, at a higher tariff rate, would not have entered into a contract anyway. On this presumption, I assumed that no one there was in this happy position and therefore would have to gracefully accept the status quo.

The meeting drew to a bad-tempered conclusion and I had a short conversation with Sidney and Roger before I left. They thanked me for intervening and asked which guesthouse I owned and what I had done prior to that.

A couple of days later, I had a telephone call from Roger inviting Gill and myself over to Folkestone for lunch as he had a proposition to put to me. When we met he said that they had been considering employing someone on a consultancy basis to grade all the hotels that they dealt with throughout the UK. The thinking behind this was that instead of one tariff rate for all, higher standard accommodation would benefit from a supplement paid for by the guest. Furthermore, because they were experiencing high demand, they needed new hotels inspected and 'brought on stream'. He said that he and his father felt that with my background in management I fitted the bill, if I was interested. The package offered was fifty pounds per week (a lot of money then) an expense account that would be sufficient to allow me to stay in the best hotels in each resort and a 'Gold Pass' for British Rail which gave me first-class travel everywhere.

Needless to say, I jumped at the chance. I spent the next six to eight months travelling all over the UK, from Cornwall to Scotland and to the east and west coasts.

I had always enjoyed train travel, ever since a youth hostelling trip to the Trossachs when I was still at school. On that occasion, we had to sleep on pallets in the guard's van, so travelling first class, including sleeper journeys and dining, was a completely different experience. The food in first class was always of a high standard, but what I particularly remember is that they always seemed to have fine clarets and some of the best Stilton that I have eaten. It is very difficult to get good Stilton now, the taste seems to be for something creamier than hitherto and without the crumbly texture. There is also a tendency to wrap everything in cling film which makes cheese sweat and, certainly with Stilton, turns it sour.

Travelling like this was also, without doubt, a different experience to one trip I had made to Edinburgh when I was about twenty. On that occasion, I had hitchhiked up from Eastbourne to see a friend and having eventually found him working over on the west coast, had travelled back by coach – twelve hours from Glasgow to London.

On the way up, somewhere near Nottingham, I had managed to get a lift with a long-distance lorry driver who was going as far as Aberdeen. However, he said that he always stayed overnight in Newcastle and that he could drop me off there for me to carry on or, if I wanted to stay, he would take me to Edinburgh the next day. As it was getting late, I chose the latter option and we eventually stopped at his usual accommodation. It looked like a bit of a doss house, the room had three metal bunks for six people but it was perfectly clean and we had a very good breakfast the next morning.

I caused some amusement to my lorry driver acquaintance when he and a friend returned when I was already in bed. I had read somewhere that when staying in this type of establishment, it was a good idea to put one's shoes under the feet of the bed – so making it difficult for them to be stolen. The two lorry drivers seemed to find this riotously funny and were of the unshakeable opinion that no self-respecting tramp would consider wearing my footwear!

I remember the cost for bed and breakfast being less than one pound.

The usual procedure with SAGA was that I would travel to my destination by rail, usually sleeper journeys on the longer runs, pick up a hire car on arrival and book into my hotel.

I stayed in some very nice hotels during my travels; two I remember in particular were The Grand Hotel in Scarborough and The Turnberry on the west coast of Scotland. The Grand I remember because the only other guests were the famous Leeds football team of the time and although I do not follow football now, I did then, so it was interesting to meet them all. The Turnberry, which was a fairly luxurious four-star hotel, was occupied by me and two other guests, probably reps of some description, who had managed to find their way there in the depths of winter. Having met in the bar, we went into the cavernous dining room together and on two of us ordering roast sirloin, a huge silver trolley was wheeled in front of us with what looked like a whole sirloin on it. The waiter kept carving and we kept eating, but we appeared to make no impression on it at all.

Another slightly bizarre experience was a trip that I had to make to the Isle of Arran. The crossing from Ardrossan was very rough and the only other passenger was a Pakistani Muslim. On our arrival in Brodick, one of the crew asked if we would mind helping them unload as they were short staffed. We did help but it struck me as somewhat surreal to be unloading a ferry in a howling gale, in the company of a Muslim in traditional dress.

I was then stuck on Arran for two nights as the weather deteriorated and it was thought too rough to attempt a return crossing.

I don't know what happened to my fellow passenger.

One weekend in February/March, when I had been in Scotland for a couple of weeks, I arranged to meet Gill in York. She had booked us into an hotel in the centre, which, on our arrival from either end of the country, turned out to be a dump. We left and took a room in The Royal Station Hotel, a British Rail hotel with lovely views. Everything about it was wonderful, the food and wine, the room with a view of the old wall and Minster; and a bath so large that we could practically swim about in it together. We spent our time exploring the city, the Minster and Shambles and walking round the medieval wall. When we weren't out and about or dining, we were in bed making love, as of course we hadn't seen each other for two or three weeks. Unfortunately, all good things must come to an end and on the Monday morning we had to part on York station, me heading north and Gill, south, rather like the scene from *Brief Encounter*.

The company (SAGA) must have been pleased with what I did, as at the end of the agreed contract I was asked if I would consider staying on, on a permanent basis. I gave it a lot of thought but in the end decided against it. There were a number of reasons for this, not least because I missed Gill when I was away but I also knew that being employed rather than self-employed was not what I wanted. Furthermore, the edge would be taken off my salary by having to employ extra staff in the guesthouse to replace me.

Chapter Fourteen
Summer 1974

I had a drink with old Fred Marshall, my solicitor, and he asked what I was going to do now that I had sold the restaurant and finished my stint with SAGA. I said that I quite fancied something like business sales or estate agency. He mentioned another client of his, an estate agent, who could be interested in taking a partner.

I met Alan Diprose (Oscar) for the first time at the beginning of June in the Eastbourne Conservative Club. Oscar had an estate agency in the centre of town, called John Allan & co. I had called in there once after some details on a property and I have to say, I wasn't very impressed. The sole occupant was a woman of about sixty puffing away at a cigarette with a pile of dog ends, at least two feet high, in an ashtray on her desk. However, I hit it off with Alan straight away, he was a gregarious person who was to figure in my life probably more than any other of my friends.

We entered into a partnership agreement in June 1974. Initially I paid him a fee of £300 plus a monthly rent for the use of his office facilities and secretary, in order to proceed with the sale of businesses only. Fortunately, Fag Ash Lil, she of the two-foot-high pile of dog ends, had gone.

Someone, I forget who, referred to us as 'the odd couple' after the film and TV series of the time. Alan certainly had many of the traits of Oscar and the nickname stuck. One incident that comes to mind is when a couple came into the agency to enquire about a property we had for sale. Flipping through the filing cabinet, with the couple looking over my shoulder, I suddenly came across a half-eaten turkey drumstick! Needless to say, we didn't see them again. I was never really Felix but on that and a number of other occasions, I could see how easy it would be to become like him.

Oscar was a heavy drinker, not an alcoholic and I never, in all the years I knew him, saw him drunk, but a bottle of scotch a day man nevertheless. I had never really drunk whisky but joined him anyway and frequently became paralytic. After a couple of years of getting myself into all sorts of scrapes, I gave it up as not my drink and discovered gin.

After a couple of months – probably when we were out on one of these benders, I can't remember – I agreed to pay Alan £2000 for a full partnership. It wasn't worth that figure and as property had slumped, there was never much chance of my recouping it. But it did teach me a valuable lesson; and that was to always keep a clear head when negotiating business deals. I used this to great advantage with Oscar later in life.

The Sussex Hotel and Making New Friends

Most of our friends had left Eastbourne again. Denton was now married and living in Devon, Philip and Deane were in Nottingham, Richard and Jill had split up and divorced and Bill and Eve had moved to Liverpool. Although we saw all of them fairly often it was not the same as having friends in town.

"I hear that there are new landlords at The Sussex," said Oscar one day towards the end of 1974. "Shall we go and check them out?" The Sussex Hotel was one of our watering holes, although we used it infrequently. The others were The Hurst Arms, where we could usually drink until about three p.m. The Bowls Club, which opened at five p.m. and in between these times, any bar on any train that was stationary in Eastbourne Station – Oscar having been a steward on the trains when he was younger and therefore knowing all the staff. Another venue was the back of Leeson's Butchers in Terminus Road, where Ray Leeson would cook us all steaks and drink could be had from The Gildredge pub next door.

The Sussex opened up a whole new chapter in our lives. The new landlords, Philip and Christine were drinkers to be ranked alongside Oscar, that is to say, in a class of their own. Philip was quickly renamed Basil as an hotelier very much in the mode of Basil Fawlty. But whereas Basil could hold his drink, Christine couldn't and frequently fell off her barstool, where we would ungallantly leave her while we continued playing 'spoof'. On one notorious occasion, Basil had picked Christine up and placing her in the lift, pressed the button to send her up to the fourth floor where they had a flat. He then returned to the bar, having given no consideration to the unlikelihood of Christine being able to exit the lift herself. Sure enough, about ten minutes later, in came one of the hotel guests and said to Basil, "There is a woman slumped asleep on the floor of the lift."

To which Basil replied, "Oh don't worry, it's only my wife," and then carried on with his conversation.

About September or October 1975, I had managed to get a sale on our guesthouse through the agency. The price agreed was £14,000 but we had to buy the purchasers' house in Hampden Park to facilitate the deal. Round about the same time, Oscar and myself had decided the estate agency had to go, as property sales had virtually dried up. One of the businesses we had on the books was a dry cleaner's, James Valet Service. I could see it was a profitable business and although we knew nothing about dry cleaning, we knew someone who did, Ken, who we had met in The Sussex along with his friends – a very loquacious Paddy named Danny and an equally verbose Welshman named John – worked for Sketchly Dry Cleaners. We put the proposition of a move to him and he was very keen, we went ahead and bought the business, for I think about £8,000. It was a very good move as not only did it provide us all with a good income, but it also curtailed the amount of drinking time available to us!

In the meantime, about November 1975, the sale on Elmscroft went through and we moved to Hampden Park, into the house we had purchased. Gill and I had already decided on our next move, which was to buy the guesthouse next door to Elmscroft – Rosforde. This had just come onto the market at about £25,000 freehold. We knew it to be a very good business, with no major works to be carried out, and far superior in its furnishings and fittings to Elmscroft. We moved in in March 1976.

Through the next two or three years, our finances started to improve substantially and our new circle of friends started to widen. We met Ray and Barbara (Ray was the manager of the local Information Bureau) Graham and Ann and Len and Mary, fellow hoteliers, and many, many more. Oscar had left his wife and met a divorced teacher, Kay. They, along with Basil and Christine and Ray and Barbara became our close friends.

Our social life improved dramatically, with weekends away and barbecues and dinner parties. We also used a restaurant called The White Friars quite a lot, which was out in the country. Although it was English owned, it was run by a very charismatic Italian called Giovanni, along with a number of other Italians, including his brother.

A weekend that sticks in my mind was in May 1977, when we spent a few days down in Cornwall, in Rock, before it became fashionable. Basil and Christine had rented a bungalow for a week which had views across to Padstow and steps from the garden down to the beach. We went to stay with them from Friday to Monday, meeting up in a pub in Wadebridge at lunchtime. Obviously the drinking started there and didn't really stop. On the Saturday night we had dinner in Padstow in a restaurant called The Blue Lobster and by Sunday morning, Gill and I, feeling jaded, were planning an escape for the day. We said to Basil and Christine that we wanted to go for a walk to give Morphine a good run. Basil thought this a good idea and suggested the four of us, along with the three dogs, walk along the beach to the pub. I pointed out the pub was only three or four hundred yards away and was therefore not really our idea of a walk. We agreed to meet up for dinner in the evening, so off we went.

We had a perfect day, exploring two or three little fishing villages and ending up in Boscastle where we had crab sandwiches and tea sitting in the garden of a café by the river. In the afternoon, we explored the area that Thomas Hardy had written about in his semi-autobiographical *A Pair of Blue Eyes*. Along with Dickens, Hardy was one of my favourite authors and we spent several weekends in Dorset discovering the places mentioned in various novels.

By the time we returned to the bungalow, Basil, who had been slightly offended at our wanting to go off on our own, had got over it and we had a very pleasant dinner together to round off the weekend.

A final anecdote in regard to The Sussex, was an incident later that same year. The Sussex was like a club, always the same people in the bar, but with longer opening hours! This was long before all day opening but there was always a selection of us 'coterie of regulars' Saturday or Sunday afternoons and late on Friday and Saturday nights. On this particular occasion me and one of my friends, Graham (Sac) had been over to France for a day and arriving back in Dover about midnight, feeling hungry, drove round trying to find somewhere to eat on the way but without success. However, on entering Eastbourne at about two a.m. we thought it worth checking out The Sussex. Sure enough, we could see chinks of light through the bar curtains and so rang the front door bell. As known faces, we were ushered into the bar by the night porter, to be greeted by an exuberant Basil, who first plied us with drinks and then fed us with bacon sandwiches.

There must have been twenty regulars still in there at that time of night!

We had decided to sell Rosforde at the end of the 1978 season as we wanted something either larger or in a better position, or preferably both.

Some friends of ours had managed a hotel called The Park View and had shown us over the property. We had also heard through the grapevine that the proprietors intended putting it up for sale. The Park View came on the market in the spring of 1979 at £50,000 and as we had sold Rosforde for £36,000, I knew there would be no problem in raising the funds from the bank. Unfortunately, however, when we approached the vendors, they said that as property has started to increase in value, they were staying put until October. Come October, having not seen anything else that we fancied, we had to pay £75,000. This increase in cost was a bit of a blow but as the dry cleaner's was doing particularly well, we weren't too bothered. We moved into The Park View on October 5th.

Chapter Fifteen
Park View Years 1979-89

Park View, which faced the Congress Theatre, was a different proposition to our two previous guesthouses. It had its own car park and garden to the rear with access from the garden into a two acre private lawn which was surrounded by other hotels. Each property owned a section of these communal gardens. It was not only ideal for young children, Rupert was seven, although Karen was now sixteen, but great for barbecues during the summer.

We had seen from our numerous visits that the hotel, though small, had massive potential. Although there were only fifteen bedrooms, all were of a sufficient size to install bathrooms and there was room for a lift, which along with a car park were the most important facilities. There was also room for a bar once a licence had been granted.

Gill and I, for all our drive and willingness to work (and I believe we both had that in abundance) were never particularly single minded. We felt that if we didn't do something this year, then it would probably get done the next. Very often this meant that if we wanted a holiday with the children, to such places as the Seychelles or Cyprus, or a new car, then some necessary expenditure in the hotel had to be postponed. No doubt with a different attitude we could have progressed financially a lot more quickly than we did.

However, it should be said that we never shirked work or a problem. Whilst carrying out the renovations to upgrade the hotel, it was necessary to take out three chimney breasts within the top three storeys of the building. The builders, having taken these out and having installed the RSJs and made good, were left with three huge piles of rubble, one on each floor level. Much discussion ensued as to how this was to be transported down to the skip at the front of the property. A chute was suggested, dismissed as too expensive, throwing it out the window, dismissed as too dangerous. There was a lot of scratching of heads, smoking and peering up from below, or down from above, but all to no avail. I could see that at this rate it was going to cost more in discussion than in any method of moving it, not excluding a crane. That night, Gill and I, with the aid of a shovel and four metal buckets, moved it all down. Gill filled two empty buckets while I ran down the stairs with two full ones. I did this two hundred and seventy times (five hundred and forty buckets), it took us about six hours.

The following day the builders, after their initial surprise, were to say the least, a bit sheepish.

Our repayments on the fifty thousand borrowing were hefty at ten thousand per annum (ten percent flat rate) over ten years. That sort of interest rate seems a joke now but that's what we had to pay at the time. However, by the spring of 1984, we had carried out all the work necessary to transform the Park View from a large guesthouse into a small, but good, three-star standard hotel. The turnover increased massively.

One of the nightmares of a hotelier is the fire alarm activating in the middle of the night, worse by far of course if there is a fire, but fortunately this never happened to us. However, one night the alarms did go off; you are woken with your nerves jangling but knowing that it is your responsibility to do something about it. Our procedure was that I would check the panel to see which zone of the hotel had a problem. If it was the bar area or dining room (rather than a bedroom) then once I had established that nothing was amiss, Gill would go upstairs reassuring the guests. The usual cause of these false alarms was possibly dust or a fly entering the detector. On this occasion, after my checking, Gill flew upstairs shouting, "Not to worry, it's only a fly". I followed her up from our flat and on the ground floor found Herr Stevens, one of a couple of German guests, gazing up the staircase as if mesmerised. I looked up and saw that Gill had thrown on a short suede coat, but nothing else! At breakfast, Herr Stevens announced with a twinkle in his eye that he would set the fire alarms off again that night and stand guard at the foot of the staircase.

I had noticed over the years that I had known Gill, that although she thought her mother eccentric, she did not lack eccentricity herself.

Quite apart from running up a flight of stairs naked from the hips down, or storming through the town on a Saturday night dressed in a low cut Nell Gwynne dress and mob cap, there had been a number of other incidents. Two or three worth mentioning are:

Once, when standing in the dining room talking to some guests, she had pulled out of a pocket what she thought to be a handkerchief, and proceeded to blow her nose with one of Rupert's long school socks which hung down somewhat in the fashion of a grey trunk. She didn't notice until the whole room was convulsed with laughter. She frequently, by mistake, took off with other people's trolleys when shopping in supermarkets and on one occasion was chased round Sainsbury's by a member of staff shouting, "Madam, madam!" On being stopped, she found herself to be pushing a trolley piled six feet high with broken down cardboard boxes!

One final thing (for the time being anyway) was an occasion when I was standing outside a shop reading a newspaper whilst waiting for Gill. I heard her say, "Are you ready to go?"

A male voice replied, "I certainly am, if you are darling." She had come out of the shop but still looking in the window, had slipped her arm through the arm of a complete stranger wearing a similar coat to mine.

The Park View years were good years. We had barbecues in the summer for thirty or forty friends and in the winter, dinner parties for up to twenty. Cyprus became a regular venue a couple of times a year with a variety of friends. We had several weekends in Majorca and went back to the Seychelles again in 1986, although we were a little bored on that occasion as we had decided that lying about on a beach was not really our thing. Another reason for avoiding the Seychelles was the cost. Although it had probably cost more to get there in 1981 than in 1986, in 1986 the cost of eating out had sky rocketed. The main reason for this we were told, was that the government had doubled or tripled the taxes on alcohol. Whether or not this was the case, I have no idea, but to dine in a restaurant now cost over £100, whereas only five years earlier it had averaged about £40.

Majorca holiday 1982

In October 1982, we spent an enjoyable holiday in Majorca with Ray and Barbara and their daughter Karen, and Pam (Barbara's sister) and her two boys. The three boys were all around the same age (ten/eleven years) and got on well together.

We had all booked into what turned out to be a fairly downmarket hotel in Cala Bona, occupied mainly by German holidaymakers. The food wasn't particularly good so we ate out in a little restaurant on the harbour most nights. However, on one memorable occasion, displayed on an easel in reception, as it always was, was the dinner menu for that night, egg and chips! As the three boys and me all fancied this meal we decided to reserve a table for that evening. At breakfast, I asked the Spanish head waiter (Thomas), who other than being not as smart, resembled the head waiter in *Duty Free*, a popular TV programme of that time, if he would reserve a table for all nine of us; handing him the equivalent of five pounds at the same time. Thomas, although always cheerful and obliging, was fairly scruffy, usually with a frayed shirt and stained waiter's jacket.

Arriving at the dining room door that evening, we were met by a transformed and resplendent Thomas in a clean, white shirt, completely intact round the collar and cuffs, and a spotless, laundered waiter's jacket. Watched in amazement by the other diners, we were led ceremoniously (in a crocodile) to our table which was neatly laid up, with linen napkins instead of the usual paper, a glass water jug rather than plastic, the two bottles of wine I had ordered and bizarrely, a Christmas cracker at each place setting. The egg and chips, which the other diners appeared to be helping themselves to from a buffet, was served to us on huge silver platters, personally supervised by the redoubtable Thomas.

We got to know quite a few Germans fairly well, in particular a couple, Wolfram and his wife; Wolfram being a huge bloke of about six foot six. We had some enjoyable, but fairly heavy, drinking sessions with groups of them. Pam probably spent the most time with them and I remember on one occasion on our joining a few of them, including a fairly inebriated Pam, much to their amusement, she turned to us and said, "They like drong strinks, this lot."

There were quite a few fishing boats which plied in and out of the small harbour and we had noticed that a large part of their catch was a type of shiny, blue fish. Having been told by the owners of the restaurant that we used, how it was normally prepared, we arranged to have it for dinner one of the nights.

The day that we were due to have the blue fish in the evening, Gill and I hired a car and with Rupert, went off to explore the island on our own. We found a tiny cove with just one beach bar, that we later renamed Cala Sangria. We bought a jug of Sangria from the bar and along with some rolls and ham, had this for our lunch. Unwisely we had another jug and although I didn't know what was in it, it was definitely a 'drong strink'! After lunch, Rupert and I had a swim and left Gill sunbathing topless on the beach. Some half-hour later I saw that Gill was surrounded by seven or eight fishermen. Walking back up the beach towards them, I saw that Gill was lying back in just her bikini bottom, chatting away to them quite unconcernedly. On my arrival, they started to drift off but with lots of grinning and cries of 'hermoso!' and 'bella'.

Gill, who had finished the second jug of sangria in our absence, was chattering and grinning inanely. Putting her into the car, I drove back to Cala Bona and pulling up outside the hotel, sent Rupert to find Ray to give me a hand. When Ray appeared we got Gill out of the car and standing either side of her for support, we marched into the hotel foyer. Various generations of the family that owned the hotel, always sat in a line on a couch in reception, watching with curiosity and some bemusement, the comings and goings of their guests. We tried to walk through as nonchalantly as possible, greeting them with the usual 'hola' but probably resembled people in a three-legged race with an extra person added. Nonetheless, we thought that we were doing quite well until we heard a booming voice shout, "Ah! There is a problem with Gill!" From out of the bar appeared the giant Wolfram and his wife. Had there been any chance of discretion, it was now blown, as with a shout of "Bistoffen. No problem," he scooped Gill up like a small doll and carried her upstairs with Ray, me and his wife trooping behind. On reaching our room he gently laid the giggling Gill, who kept repeating, 'Don't make me eat the blue fish', on our bed. We three men were then shooed out of the room by his wife who said she would look after her.

We never did get to eat the blue fish that evening, although everyone else said that they enjoyed it.

We employed quite a few part time staff at Park View, among them being three girls who more or less started together at the age of fourteen or fifteen. Nicky, Diana and Helen worked with us throughout their teenage years and continued to do so until they had finished at university. They were great fun, lively and gregarious, and when they were older would help out at barbecues and generally join in.

A memorable evening early on, was a medieval feast that we organised with two of our friends who owned a larger hotel, The Norfolk. Graham (Sac) and me had been discussing holding some medieval banquets in his large function room but fortunately decided that it may be a good idea to have a trial run before we started charging for them. We booked my sister, Mal, and her band to play and about sixty friends were invited.

We arranged a five or six course menu with the main course being racks of lamb and beef. Everything was, of course, free including vast quantities of drink. I, being the chef, was in charge of the kitchen, while Sac officiated upstairs. Initially everything ran smoothly. We had huge pots of meat broth and Sussex smokies ready for the first two courses, all the vegetables prepared and the pudding ready for cooking. However, when we switched on the antiquated ovens to bring them up to temperature for the dozens of racks of lamb and beef to be cooked, nothing happened to two of them, only one worked. There was nothing to be done but take the majority of the trays of lamb and beef round to the Park View kitchens to be cooked there. I told Sac that we would have to delay the start of the meal, which with hindsight was not a sensible thing to do, as all the guests were being fed copious amounts of free wine and mead.

The two hotels were some three or four hundred yards apart, so we had to organise relays of people, all in medieval dress, to run backwards and forwards with the trays of uncooked and then cooked meat. None of us could drive as we had all, already, drunk too much, but were sufficiently sober to know that a Robin Hood or Maid Marian, or knight in armour driving, possibly erratically, would soon be picked up.

We finally started serving the meal at about ten p.m. instead of eight thirty as planned. By the time I took my place at the table at about eleven p.m., everyone appeared to be absolutely paralytic. Food was being thrown backwards and forwards, sword fights were in progress, two or three people were comatose under tables and the King, Ray, who seemed to be more riotous than anyone and by now had gained a quite astonishingly enlivened idea of kingship, was arguing vociferously with the Queen, Barbara.

The 'merriment' continued for another two or three hours, until there were now more people in a prone position than upright. The King and Queen were still shouting at each other and Barbara was soaked in wine that Ray had obviously poured over her head. In my trying to remonstrate with Ray and calm him down, I got a punch in the eye for my trouble. Feeling a little aggrieved, I had him unceremoniously thrown out still in his king's apparel and complete with crown and silly turned-up shoes.

At about three a.m., feeling a little guilty at having my friend thrown out, Gill, Barbara and I went in search of him. I guessed where he would be, as being the manager of The Information Bureau, he usually homed in there. We knocked on the door at the front of the office, but gained no response. It then occurred to us, that being dressed the way he was, all of us having changed at the Park View, he was unlikely to have any keys with him. We walked around the back into Wish Road and, sure enough, there was a pair of legs, complete with turned-up shoes, sticking out of a large dustbin. Between us we managed to extricate him by tipping over the bin and while I held it, the two girls hauled him out.

We probably made a lot of noise and I have since often wondered if anyone in the surrounding properties had woken up and looked out of the window to see Robin Hood and Maid Marian, along with a queen, pulling a king out of a refuse bin. I imagine that they probably would have thought it a dream and just gone back to bed!

Needless to say, we gave up any idea of medieval feasts after that.

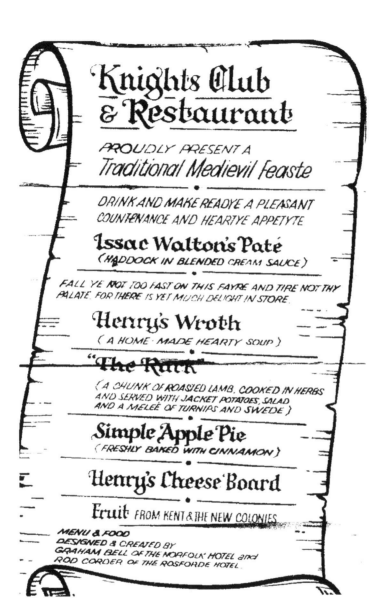

Knights Club & Restaurant

PROUDLY PRESENT A
Traditional Medievil Feaste

• • •

DRINK AND MAKE READYE A PLEASANT
COUNTENANCE AND HEARTYE APPETYTE

Issac Walton's Paté
(HADDOCK IN BLENDED CREAM SAUCE)

• • •

FALL YE NOT TOO FAST ON THIS FAYRE AND TIRE NOT THY
PALATE, FOR THERE IS YET MUCH DELIGHT IN STORE.

Henry's Wroth
(A HOME-MADE HEARTY SOUP)

• • •

"The Rack"
(A CHUNK OF ROASTED LAMB, COOKED IN HERBS
AND SERVED WITH JACKET POTATOES, SALAD
AND A MELEÉ OF TURNIPS AND SWEDE)

• • •

Simple Apple Pie
(FRESHLY BAKED WITH CINNAMON)

• • •

Henry's Cheese Board

• • •

Fruit FROM KENT & THE NEW COLONIES

MENU & FOOD
DESIGNED & CREATED BY
GRAHAM BELL OF THE NORFOLK HOTEL and
ROD CORDER OF THE ROSFORDE HOTEL

The Red Roof Debacle

We had purchased Alan's share of the dry cleaners in about 1980 as he wanted to buy a pub with Kay, which they did, and although the cleaner's was an excellent income, we sold it in 1984 in order to fund the works at the hotel.

To complete the major refurbishment that we had carried out, we decided that it was necessary to have a new roof.

All the work had been overseen by a cousin of Gill's, Ian. Although Ian was a little dubious, I gave the contract for the new roof to an acquaintance who happened to be a fellow member of The Royal Golf Club. He made a complete hash of it and, given a second crack at it, did no better. I ordered him and his men off the site and asked Hall & Co (a local firm) to come in and do the work properly, which they did.

However, on our return from a day trip on the Thames with Alan, Kay and the children, my parents who had been left in charge of the hotel, showed us an article in the local paper which said that we were to be served with an enforcement notice to remove the new, red tiled roof, as we had not obtained planning consent for a change of cladding from slate.

This was the first we had heard of anything about it, although some jumped-up little creep had already informed the local press.

I telephoned Ian, who said that he had been informed that although consent wasn't needed for domestic properties, it was for commercial properties. He added that there were several hotels and guest houses in the town that, over the years, had changed their roof cladding without consent and without adverse consequences. He had put this to the planning officer that he had spoken to, who had agreed with him but said that it had only really been taken up because a local Liberal councillor, who was a member of the planning committee and at the same time a member of the conservation committee was pushing it.

From there on it became a fight.

It would cost us £10,000 to take off the tiles and re-slate the roof. The scaffolding, a major part of the cost, had only been removed the previous week.

Our choice was to opt for a public enquiry or a decision taken at the DOE in London. We opted for the enquiry as we felt that we could get public opinion behind us. We managed to have it aired on Southern Television and in local papers and were helped tremendously by the local MP, Ian Gow. Ian Gow, who was later to be killed by a suspected terrorist bomb, put an enormous amount of time and effort into it.

We identified twenty to thirty hotels and guesthouses that had changed their roof coverings in recent years without consent, including one belonging to one of the Liberal councillors who was objecting to ours! More importantly, at both Rosforde and Elmscroft, our previous guesthouses, we had renewed the roofs of both during our time there.

Public support was overwhelmingly on our side, both from the publicity drummed up in the press and on TV and from a petition maintained outside the hotel by various friends.

The public enquiry, which was held at the town hall, lasted for two days. The inspector found in our favour, mainly as already mentioned because of the incompetence on the council's part and public support for us, as shown by the thousands of signatures on our petition. The Liberal councillor who had created the original furore, stated that it was in a conservation area, when in fact it wasn't. Having had this mistake pointed out to him, he then tried to argue that as it was the council's intention to include this road in the conservation area, it amounted to the same thing. The inspector, with noticeable irritation, said that it was not the same thing as he was there to deal with the facts as they were at present and not to consider what might or might not happen in the future.

One of the planning officers, to bolster their argument against the thirty-odd properties that we had identified as having a change of roof cladding without consent, chose, unbeknown to him, our two previous guesthouses, Elmscroft and Rosforde, to illustrate a point. He said that, among others, he had inspected those two properties and that in fact, neither had the original slate replaced with tiles but had merely been Turnerised. When I pointed out that we had owned both properties mentioned and had re-roofed both ourselves, I saw a flicker of a smile cross the inspector's face and I was then fairly sure that we had won.

Running a small hotel, especially of the standard of the Park View and where the proprietors are very much hands-on, can be very hard work. Our day would commence at six a.m. and although effectively we were finished by about 9.30 p.m., when dinner was over, we were still on call until about midnight. Our way round this was to play as hard as we worked, something you can continue doing in your thirties and forties.

The barbecues mentioned earlier were held on Sunday afternoon. After cooking and serving breakfast and Sunday lunch for some thirty-five people, we, along with Rupert and Karen's help and some of the staff, would set up trestle tables and chairs in the garden and by about four p.m., light up two huge barbecues on which Ray and I would cook for the forty-plus invited friends.

In those days, hotel guests seemed to be happy enough with just Sunday lunch and then salads and sandwiches in the bar in the evening. One or more of the girls would be on duty for this so leaving us free for the evening. Very often by about eight p.m., if a few people had drifted off, a nucleus of about ten or twelve of us would drive over to The Tiger Inn at East Dene to finish the evening there. Jim, the landlord at that time, always looked slightly apprehensive when we landed, but never more so than when he saw Rudi, a Dutch friend of ours, who was particularly exuberant. Rudi would invariably start the community singing, usually with *Tulips from Amsterdam* as a precursor.

Friday nights were another occasion when we could let off steam. In those days, most guests would leave on a Saturday, so Friday night was effectively the end of another week. Gill would oversee dinner while I wrote out the accounts for the morning. I drank quite a lot then and would probably polish off three or four large vodkas whilst I was in the office working. When dinner was completed about nine to nine thirty p.m., Gill would come down and we would sit in the garden listening to music and drinking wine. Unless there was an emergency, whoever was on the bar always managed to shield us from guests on a Friday night.

Saturday morning, 6 am, we were up and ready to face another week!

When Rupert was a little older, perhaps ten or eleven onwards, each summer he and I would spend a few days camping out in the country where some friends owned a smallholding. It was quite close to a restaurant called The Smugglers Wheel, which our friend, Giovanni and his brother had bought in about 1983. They had asked if Gill and I would be interested in a partnership with them prior to purchasing it but unfortunately we had used up all our funds on refurbishing the hotel. However, we and many of our friends were regular customers and when Rupert and I camped, we would often cycle over and have lunch there, sitting in a lovely garden. It was quite an expensive restaurant, with a very high standard of food and the friendly but efficient service that Italians are so good at. On one occasion, Rupert and I sitting outside in our shorts, having just finished a lobster salad and a bottle of Pouilly Fume, were playing a game of spoof for another drink with Giovanni, when out came a party of people who were just leaving. As they passed us, we heard one of the ladies say, "Giovanni must have started doing bar snacks!" Oh, the snobbery and angst of some of the middle classes!

A sad time at Park View was in January 1985, when Morphine, our faithful and entertaining dog, died. He was about seventeen, so a fair age and had been a good friend and at times protector to Karen and Rupert. When Karen was about eighteen, she used to take Morph down to the pub in the town where she would meet her friends. By all accounts he became quite a celebrity there and had his own bowl filled with half a bitter. We, in turn, never had to worry about Karen walking home late whilst accompanied by Morph.

When I say Morph was entertaining, there were many times when he was; one incident in particular sticks in my mind. When Karen and Rupert were younger, we were walking up on the Downs and had sat down behind a hedge for a picnic. We heard a number of people walking past on the other side, who then stopped some forty or fifty yards past us, but still out of sight. Morphine went to investigate and from the conversation drifting over the hedge, it was apparent that the group were having a picnic too. We heard a female voice exclaim, "Oh, what a lovely dog," and then. "Look he has a name tag – Morphine – that's a funny name but isn't he handsome?"

Unfortunately things went downhill from there. We heard another voice, male this time, shout, "He's got the cheese – Morphine, come back." Then a general hue and cry started up, we could hear Morphine racing through an adjacent wood pursued by a number of people. We kept quiet and hoped that Morph wouldn't lead the pack to us. Eventually, he reappeared, licking his lips, and we made our exit as quickly as possible.

A final mention of Morph was an occasion early on at the Park View, sometime in the winter, probably about 1980. I had been out for a drink with Ken (our manager at the dry cleaner's) and we were later joined by Ken's wife, June and a friend of hers. We were eventually turfed out of the pub about eleven thirty p.m. and I thought it would be a good idea to continue drinking back at The Park View, as we were not yet open for the summer. Gill obviously didn't think this a good idea and shortly after our arrival, came storming down from our bedroom, flung open the bar door and as I went to meet my 'little treasure', hit me with such force that I ended up flat on my back. She then raced back up to the bedroom with me in hot pursuit and, unbeknown to us, Morph, who had heard the commotion and broken free from downstairs, in pursuit of me. Just as I grabbed Gill in the bedroom, I felt a pair of gnashers grip my arm and there was Morph hanging on for grim death. I swung round a couple of times in an effort to make him let go and all of a sudden he did so, flying off backwards towards the open door at a height of about five feet. As misfortune would have it, just as he was exiting the room, Ken came in, having chased us upstairs too. They both went back down in a flurry of paws, arms and legs, accompanied by barks from Morph and yelps from Ken. Fortunately no one was any the worse for wear, but Morph was known for a long time after as Krypton (the flying dog).

A further final mention of Morph.

This was Gill's twenty-third birthday.

We had managed to accumulate enough money to buy two steaks for a birthday dinner and as a further present (unbeknown to Gill) I had ordered a single rose to be delivered. That morning we had a row over something or other but when the rose arrived, I took it down to the kitchen as a peace offering. It was in an attractive presentation box, laying on a bed of silky material and covered with cellophane. The 'light of my life' was chopping cabbage with a large chopping knife. Without saying a word, she split the ribbon round the box, took out the rose and, after chopping it into small pieces, with a final flourish scraped it into the waste bin.

We didn't speak for the rest of the day and, having served dinner to the guests, at about eight p.m. I went to the pub for a drink. Returning an hour or so later, Gill had obviously calmed down and apologised for chopping up her present. However, whilst still in a temper, she had cooked and eaten her steak, but giving me a loving kiss said that she would now cook mine and we could have a bottle of wine to celebrate her birthday. Off she went to the pantry, but no sign of a steak, just an empty plate! The redoubtable Morphine had obviously decided that if I wasn't there to eat the steak, then he would do so!

The Dragon

Our children were now growing up. Karen helped in the hotel and so did Rupert, although he was still at school.

Karen was a great help in the hotel and in fact had been in helping to look after Rupert when he was young; although on one occasion when he was about three and annoying her, she knocked him out! From the age of about sixteen or seventeen, she became known as The Dragon. She acquired this appellation, by which she is still known today, from a group of young musicians who were staying in the hotel. They were with (I think) the London Symphony Orchestra and were late for breakfast. Apparently Karen had found them all practising the Superman film theme in one of their bedrooms and had demanded to know whether they were coming down for breakfast or not! Although I knew nothing about this, they scurried down to breakfast and on passing my office to enter the dining room, I heard one say, "She's a bit of all right, but a bit of a dragon."

When she was a little younger than this, perhaps about fourteen, she was the epitome of the awkward, gangly teenager. She could fall over whilst having a conversation with you and never seemed to be able to sit on the kitchen stools without falling off. She managed to tip a full catering tin of biscuits over Gill's head and would never fully replace the top on a sauce bottle. I managed to rid her of this habit one Sunday morning at breakfast. I saw that the cap of the sauce bottle was balanced in its usual precarious position. Picking up the bottle, I aimed it at The Dragon and brought it down swiftly in an arc. The top flew off and a stream of brown sauce stretched from the top of her forehead straight down her nose, reaching her chest. She laughed so much that she fell off her stool again and disappeared under the table.

One final anecdote was one of the funniest scenes that I have ever witnessed. This was before we had telephones installed in each bedroom, so for guests' use there was a public payphone positioned at the top of the staircase which led down to our private quarters. I happened to be in the bar and was aware that a lady guest was using the telephone. The front doorbell rang and I heard The Dragon thundering up the stairs to answer it. She threw open the door at the top with such force that it knocked a fire extinguisher out of its bracket on the wall; it went off. The hose managed to detach itself from its retaining clip and started swinging about like a demented snake. I rushed out of the bar, followed by two or three guests, to be met with a scene of mayhem. The hose was swinging at a furious rate and at each pass was shooting water and foam straight up the lady's skirt. She, unbelievably, was still talking on the telephone but now giving a running commentary on her predicament, whilst jumping and twirling like a dervish, trying to avoid the hose. The Dragon was flat on the floor, covered in foam and laughing uncontrollably.

In 1987, we came close to purchasing an hotel called Overton Grange, in Shropshire, the county where I had spent much of my youth, but although we had a sale on the Park View, for a number of reasons, we changed our minds. However, it was obvious that we were ready for a change as we both wanted something larger and we probably shouldn't have stayed at the Park View for as long as we had done.

My parents had moved down to Eastbourne in 1970 and had been a great help both in the bringing up of the children and in helping in the various guesthouses and businesses that we had had over the years. They were now living in semi-retirement in a flat we had bought for them, just round the corner from the hotel. In December 1988, they celebrated fifty years of marriage at the hotel and a lot of friends and relatives came down from Wolverhampton.

In June 1989 we sold the Park View for £360,000, a very good price, as unbeknown to us the property market was about to crash. Unfortunately, not so good of course for the purchasers, but the business itself was very sound and profitable.

Philip (with transport) ready to leave for Eastbourne April 12 1965

First date 31st May 1965

Gill and Rod, Lake District 1966

Gill, Lake District 1966

Gill, Deane, Lyn, Paul, 'Pip', Bill, Wendy, Philip 1967

Rod, Anna, Denton, Gill 1970

Our wedding 1968

Medieval Banquet

Karen aged about four

Karen and Rupert 1979

Rupert aged about four

Gill 1975

Rod 1976

THE RED ROOF VICTORY

TORIES RAP PLANNERS

By SARAH CLARKE

EASTBOURNE'S Deputy Mayor, Tory, Mr Derek Ellis, has described the result of the Park View Hotel's red roof appeal as a victory for common sense.

And Tory members of the borough council's planning committee strongly criticised the decision to try and force the hotel owner to remove the red tiles — a decision which led to an expensive two-day planning inquiry.

An inspector for the Department of the Environment recently upheld hotel proprietor Mr Rod Corder's appeal against the borough council's enforcement notice.

Borough planners had said that the red tiles on the roof should be removed as they had been put up without planning permission.

At a meeting of the planning committee Mr Ellis said, 'Common sense has prevailed in the end.

'This was a relatively minor matter and should never have led to an appeal situation.'

Mrs Kathleen Raven (Conservative, Meads) said it had been unnecessary for the council to get involved in the expensive procedure of a two-day appeal.

Principal borough solicitor Mr Geoff Johnson said the Department of the Environment's inspector had supported the council on some grounds and his report had not set a precedent for the future.

Committee chairman Mrs Theresia Williamson said, 'I welcome the report — it gives us useful guidelines.'

The Red Roof victory

Gill 1982

Seychelles 1986

Gill and Barbara

Morphine in Cornwall

Gill in Henley 1982

Ray and Rod 1981

Oscar, Kay, Gill and Rod – Cavendish Hotel 1985

Silver Wedding, Unicorn Hotel 1993

Silver Wedding 1993

Rupert (the professional) keeping a beady eye on Basil (the amateur) preparing lunch. Boxing Day 1992

A cartoon drawn by Ray – after my having complained to Basil about smoking while we were eating

Rod and Rupert (worse for wear) Greece 1996

Rupert and 'Dragon' Christmas 1999

Rod and 'Dragon' 2002

Gill and 'Dragon', Nottingham 2013

Gill and Road, Grindelwald (Switzerland) 2006

Basil, Christine and Gill 1998

Three of the 'quadrille', Cheryl, Benita, Gill and Lisa November 2001, leaving party, Greek restaurant

Gill, John, Barbara and Rod, Switzerland, January 2007

Yew Tree Cottage 2015

Chapter Sixteen
Two or Three Years OFF

For a short time we moved in with my parents. Rupert was about to start sixth form college and Karen, against our better judgement, was now married.

We continued looking at other hotels and businesses but weren't in a hurry to purchase anything, as we could see property values dropping on an almost daily basis. However, two in particular are worth mentioning, not because we were particularly interested in either but because of a previous association with one and the entertainment value of the other. The first was a hotel in Eskdale and on our arriving for our appointment to view it, we realised we had been there before. Twenty-three years previously when on holiday with Denton, we had called in for a drink at lunchtime but had been refused admission on the basis that they didn't serve hippies. The hippy in question was me, with my shoulder length hair and a goatskin coat which always retained a certain odour! The other was an hotel in the Eden Valley, in between Penrith and Carlisle. Our intention was to view the property and then stop overnight somewhere on our way back south, but as the weather was pretty atrocious, we asked if we could book in there. Unbeknown to us it was Burns' Night so although they had accommodation, the restaurant was fully booked. However, the proprietors said that a couple of guests were close friends and they would telephone them and ask if they would mind sharing a table with us. This was arranged and when we came down to dinner at about eight p.m., we were introduced. Although the couple were quite a lot older than us, we hit it off straight away. He was a surveyor and had a real 'drinker's nose'. We have never had such an entertaining Burns' Night – the food was good, the pipers were good and the sixty to seventy people there were out to enjoy themselves.

Although there were several miniatures of whisky on each table, our host, the surveyor, I can't remember his name, insisted on ordering another full bottle besides the wine already ordered. He was pouring it liberally onto his haggis, saying that this was the traditional method and encouraged Gill to do the same. Gill never needs a lot of encouragement in these situations! God knows how much they drank between them. When it got to about two a.m. and people were starting to drift away, I was chatting to someone in the foyer, when looking over my shoulder he suddenly said, "There's a girl over there in high heels and a short skirt gradually sliding down the wall." I somehow knew it was Gill before turning around but before I reached her, the surveyor and his wife had managed to catch her in descent and sat her in a chair. She didn't feel too good the following morning.

In September of 1989, Gill and I decided to travel to Cyprus by car via the Bordeaux region and Italy and Greece; taking some three or four months over it. Unfortunately, we had only been away a few days and were in the south of France when, on telephoning home, I was told by my brother that our father had died. This was totally unexpected as, apart from the remnants of a cold, he had seemed perfectly healthy when we left only a few days previously. His death affected me quite a lot as I had always been close to my father, closer than I probably was to my mother. He had worked with me for most of the years we had owned the Park View and I had got to know him again after a gap of some eighteen to twenty years; since I had left home as a teenager. I regretted not spending more time with him, perhaps to have gone fishing for a few days, one of his passions, but I hadn't done so and now it was too late. However, one consolation was that in working with us over the years he was able to spend a great deal of time with the children, who he thought the world of, more than probably most grandfathers. He and Rupert, although Rupert was now just seventeen, were still great mates.

It was nice to have some time off. This was our first real break since having sold the guesthouse in March of 1979, prior to our purchase of the Park View in October that year. Although we still had the dry cleaner's to manage in the summer of 1979, at that time it felt like a break. This time, however, there were no other businesses to occupy our time so we tried to make the most of it. We had several holidays abroad, mostly in Cyprus, usually with one set of friends or another; drove down to the Bordeaux region again on a wine buying trip and spent a weekend on a boat on the Thames with our friends, Sac and Anne.

On one of the trips to Cyprus, staying with Alan and Kaye at Helios Bay Apartments on the Coral Bay road, Gill was ill for a couple of days with a stomach upset. On the third or fourth day, as she felt much better, I wandered into town on my own and ended up at one of our daytime haunts, a dark, fairly scruffy little café in the market. We had been introduced to this establishment, which was definitely not a tourist venue, by our friend, Andy, who owned a restaurant called Hondros (the fat man) in Kato Paphos. Sovvos, the owner of the café, only really catered for the market traders in those days. We once had a breakfast there at four a.m., which consisted of kebabs, particularly good sheftalia and a soup which was garnished with Sovvos' version of croutons, dry bread broken into chunks and thrown on top. All washed down with Cyprus brandy and the Greeks' sludgy apology for coffee. Cyprus brandy was a lethal concoction, one appeared to be drinking something fairly benign but it would turn on you and kick like a mule. On this occasion, whilst having a beer and kebab, I got chatting to a Belgian who said he was a chef and owned a Michelin-starred restaurant in Brussels. Finding him quite convivial, we ordered a bottle of brandy and were then soon joined by Sovvos and his two friends, this trio being known as the 'three moustachios'. Someone had painted a very good likeness of them, which now hung in Sovvos' café. More and more grilled meats kept appearing along with several more bottles of brandy, all to be as Sovvos put it 'on his head'. I vaguely remember leaving hours later when it was still light but instead of returning to the apartments decided I needed a sleep first.

As the market was now deserted, I found a convenient slab and fell asleep only to wake up to find everywhere in darkness. I managed to find my way from the market down onto the Coral Bay road, which entailed crossing a large expanse of scrubland. Paphos was not built up then as it is now and prior to the construction of the Coral Bay road, it used to be necessary to go via Chlorokas to reach Coral Bay itself. There was very little traffic as there were only two tavernas in Coral Bay but I managed to flag down a car. This turned out to be a taxi which delivered me back to the apartments, undeservedly unscathed, at no charge and with a free cigarette. I think the driver thought this a small price to pay in order to get me out of his cab!

We first went to Cyprus in 1981 and in those days, and for a good few years after, the standard of food, with a few exceptions such as Sovvos and Hondros, was pretty abysmal. Cypriot cuisine scarcely extended to more than a dozen dishes and most of these they seemed to make a hash of! I remember one restaurateur having served us an inedible rabbit casserole, thoughtfully enhanced with the rabbit's skull sitting on top, telling us how only twelve months previously he had been a goatherd but was now a 'chef' of some renown. This 'oeuvre d'art' was always written as rapid or even rabid stifado rather than rabbit on his menu. The inedibility of the dish was less to do with it not being cooked sufficiently than the bizarre addition of a jar of pickled onions complete with all the vinegar, rather than small, fresh onions. Other literary gems were 'lamb's head in oven, veal Gordon blue and salmon and brick salad'. No idea either! But there again, I can't speak Greek. On one occasion, a small party of us ordered a suckling pig in advance. This was delicious when we ate it on the appointed night, spoilt only by one of the party being served an unidentifiable bone devoid of any meat apart from what looked suspiciously like a piece of tail attached. On querying this with the goatherd, he said that it was all that was left, so somebody had to have it! Portioning something or jointing, were unknown skills to Cypriots. When one bought meat in the market, the butcher would just take part of the carcass and chop from one end to the other, the size and type of joint being determined solely by where the cleaver landed.

Another dish that the goatherd and many others managed to ruin was kleftiko. The name of this dish was said to originate from the Greek word to steal – kleptein. Thieves would steal an animal, usually goat, and cook joints of it wrapped in vine leaves in a clay oven or pit. This would allow the fat to drain away as the meat cooked slowly. The modern method was to cook the meat in foil, not usually for a sufficient length of time and then to turn the whole thing, including all the grease, onto a plate. At another restaurant, which was considered somewhat upmarket by the locals, we ordered peppered steak. What turned up was a pyramid of chopped, uncooked red and green peppers standing some six inches high on the plate. On parting these heaps with our knives and forks, we found the steaks, looking pale and unappetising underneath. One lunchtime, Gill, having ordered an omelette and being presented with something that looked like a flat pitta bread, and just as hard, I offered to show the goatherd how to cook a nice, moist, cigar-shaped version. He took me through to his kitchen and furnished me with two tiny eggs and a frying pan which must have been at least a metre in diameter.

The redeeming features of Cyprus then, were that it was relatively inexpensive, the meat was always fresh (not frozen) and the people were friendly, genuine and very hospitable.

Chapter Seventeen
The Devonshire Park Hotel

We started looking round again towards the end of the year for a new business, as we felt that property prices had probably reached rock bottom, we were wrong in this. However, having travelled up and down the country viewing various hotels, we once again, as we had in 1979, came to the conclusion that we would be better off staying in Eastbourne.

Adjacent to the Park View, were two large semi-detached Victorian properties, both run as guesthouses, each with about eighteen bedrooms. We had always thought they would make a very nice hotel as they were surrounded by their own gardens with one having a fair sized car park to one side. Both guesthouses were leasehold, the freehold being owned by the Chatsworth Estate, which was reputed to never sell off property. Another drawback was that both lessees, who although wanting to sell, had been ill-advised by some local agents who almost immediately went bankrupt thereafter, that their properties were worth astronomical sums. Two hundred thousand pounds for one and one hundred thousand for the other. Quite apart from the ludicrous valuations, I was at a loss to understand the disparity of the one hundred thousand pounds between them. They were the same size properties, both had the same length of lease remaining and were subject to the same rent revisions and there was little to choose between the condition of either. These valuations had been arrived at despite the fact the some two hundred yards away there was a twenty bedroom hotel for sale (freehold) with a better turnover, for two hundred thousand pounds. I think it is obvious as to why these particular agents went bust.

I asked Malcolm Rolfe, my solicitor of long standing, to write to The Chatsworth Estate to enquire whether they were interested in selling the freehold of the two properties. The answer was no. So I asked him to write again making an offer of three hundred thousand pounds, which was probably some fifty thousand pounds over the market price. This was snapped up immediately.

Oscar (Alan), who had now separated from Kay, and myself had long been talking about another partnership and when I approached him over this venture, he was very keen. Early in 1991, we (Gill, Alan and I) signed a new partnership agreement, purchased the freehold and agreed a loan facility with the bank of a further one hundred and fifty thousand pounds.

On the sale of the Park View, we had a capital gains tax (CGT) liability of forty thousand pounds. This, if my memory serves me correctly, we had to pay over to the Inland Revenue at the expiry of eighteen months if we had not purchased another business. However, we were still allowed a further eighteen months in which to purchase another business and if we did so, could reclaim our forty thousand pounds.

The accountant that Alan and I both used, and we were in fact his first clients in his private practice, was aware of these facts but was now a partner in a larger firm. I asked him before we bought the freehold to make sure that there would be no problems with the return of the forty thousand capital gains tax as it was not a straightforward purchase of a running business. Until the purchase of the two leases, we were in effect only landlords receiving rents and not trading as hoteliers. He assured me he had looked into it and everything was in order.

Property continued to drop in value and we made what were very generous offers for the leases, fifty thousand and twenty-five thousand but neither of these offers was accepted. I was never quite sure whether the two tenants thought these offers risible or whether they thought they could hold out for more as they knew we needed both properties. Neither seemed to realise the extent to which their properties had been allowed to deteriorate and if they didn't sell now, it was their responsibility to rectify this. Unfortunately, we didn't know quite how bad both the properties were either. We had not had a survey prior to the purchase of the freehold, simply because we knew that the tenants were responsible for all repairs and maintenance. However, because we could not reach any agreement with either lessee and as we only had a limited period of time remaining in which to claim the forty thousand capital gains tax from the collector of taxes; we employed a surveyor with the intention of serving both tenants with a Schedule of Dilapidations. When the surveys were completed, it became apparent just how much cost was involved. We were looking at tens of thousands of pounds, rough estimates from our surveyor and my builder were in the region of fifty to sixty thousand pounds. The major part of this expenditure was to treat dry rot on two or three levels of each property and several of the huge Victorian bay windows would require the insertion of RSJs to replace the rotting bressumers, which were scarcely holding up the superstructure. We could have done, but did not include the cost of replacing beautiful plaster cornices that had been taken down or the removal of internal walls (or erection of new ones) without consent, to create more bedrooms. The rooves of both properties required renewing and the stacks required attention. The cost of scaffolding alone would be nine to ten thousand.

Neither tenant was in a position to carry out these major works so were left with the unfortunate choice of accepting less for the leases now or eventually having to relinquish them. They both chose the former option, the two leases being purchased for about thirty-five thousand, which, although I am sure they would disagree, was much nearer the correct value had maintenance been carried out.

January 1992

In late January, Gill, Rupert and I moved into one side of the property. Our intention was to run this side of the property, which had been trading as a guest house, for the 1992 season while our team of builders worked on the other side, replumbing, rewiring, installing a lift shaft and bathrooms to bedrooms. A new fire alarm system was necessary, fire partitions and fire doors et cetera. We had a total budget figure of one hundred and fifty thousand pounds to cover both sides, which also included the now known maintenance figure. We knew now that this figure would not be sufficient but at least having purchased the leases in time, we would be able to reclaim our forty thousand 'CGT', or so we thought!

February 1992

I asked the accountant to request the return of our capital gains tax and at the same time instructed the builders to commence ripping out the old plumbing and wiring and cutting through five floors for the lift shaft.

I spoke to the accountant on a number of occasions over the next few weeks and each time was told the money would be returned to us soon. After a few weeks the bank started pressing to know when the CGT would appear, as the loan facility had been made on the basis of its return. I decided to telephone the Inland Revenue and having got through to the tax inspector dealing with our case, was told that not only were we not entitled to the return of the forty thousand but that he had written and informed our accountants six weeks previously. The problem was that we had not commenced trading as hoteliers on acquisition of the freehold, but had acted as landlords for some twelve months. This was precisely what I had asked the accountant to check and ascertain that there would be no difficulty reclaiming it.

We were in the depths of a serious recession, almost as bad as we experienced from 2007; the bank was jittery as hotels were going bankrupt on a daily basis. Our only redress was to sue the accountants.

Malcolm Rolfe, our solicitor, Gill and I worked tirelessly on this for the next three and a half years.

At Malcolm's suggestion, we first employed a London tax barrister, but after several thousand pounds of expenditure and having seemingly made no progress at all, it became obvious to us that we were barking up the wrong tree. We both agreed that as we accepted the tax legislation shown to us was correct and as therefore we had no argument with the Inland Revenue, it followed that we had no need of a barrister who believed that we had. What we needed was counsel to carry forward a claim against the accountants for negligence and breach of contract. As luck would have it, a Barristers' Chambers had just opened in Eastbourne only a few yards up the road from Malcolm's office. It proved to be very fortuitous for us as the barrister that we engaged from there was young and enthusiastic, grasping the situation immediately.

He and Malcolm very quickly arranged Legal Aid for us. This was essential as we no longer had any funds left and of course were now fighting the accountants' professional insurers. Up until our being granted Legal Aid, they had frustratingly almost treated us with contempt, as they obviously expected us to be pushed into bankruptcy long before we ever managed to get into court.

We opened for business as soon as we could, in May 1992, but could only trade with about twelve usable bedrooms, the other side of the property now being completely gutted. I think our turnover for that year was about twenty-six thousand pounds.

One Saturday morning in July, we received a letter from the bank freezing the hotel account. On Monday morning I appeared at the bank without an appointment and demanded to see the manager, a new manager since the loan was agreed and someone that I had only met a couple of times. Over the weekend I had decided that not only was there nothing to lose by taking an aggressive approach, as we couldn't trade with our account frozen, but that it may prove to be the most prudent anyway. I was correct. I started off by explaining the obvious fact that we could not continue if things were left as they were. When he tried to put the bank's point of view, I pretended to become angry and then ostentatiously threw a set of keys of the hotel onto his desk and said that if the bank wanted to manage yet another hotel they were welcome to do so as I was not prepared to put up with the stupidity of the situation.

The bar on the account was lifted.

As I mentioned earlier, since our purchase of the freeholds in 1990, property had continued to devalue and as we had (a) knowingly overpaid for the freehold and (b) ripped out all the services and large sections of floor on each level on one side of the property, the value now was probably one hundred and fifty thousand and falling. The bank really didn't want it so long as there was a chance of us winning our action against the accountants, which would enable them to recoup their investment.

From February 1992, we fought a three and a half year battle with the accountants' insurers. Legal Aid was taken away from us twice but each time we managed to have it reinstated. We had to sell the flat that we had bought for my parents, along with our car in an effort to keep things going. Our bank manager had a nervous breakdown (I am sure not due entirely to us) and was replaced by a 'new broom' who not only seemed more amenable but also appeared to be less afraid of head office. Over time he managed to raise a further seventy-five thousand pounds of borrowing to keep us afloat. Interest rates were at ridiculous levels, sometimes hitting fourteen and fifteen percent.

Our original claim for damages against the accountants, was of course for the loss of the forty thousand but over the years this increased annually as loss of profit on what should have been a thirty bedroom hotel, was added. The final claim was in the region of four hundred and fifty thousand pounds.

During these years it felt to Gill and I as if we had regressed twenty or so years. We were once again working as hard as we had done in our mid-twenties. I cooked breakfast for thirty guests which Gill served, she then washed up, cleaned rooms and spent the rest of the day in the office, while I worked as a builder's labourer in the adjacent 'derelict' side of the property. In the evening, we cooked and served dinner for the guests, washed up and served in the bar. Our working day stretched from five thirty a.m. until midnight and at the end of the 1992 season we produced a risible turnover.

We had no money for leisure and no car but as we had very little spare time it didn't seem to matter that much. With a wide circle of friends we still had a good, though financially much toned down, social life. A lot of our friends were also finding things difficult in what was an increasingly severe recession. Holidays, weekends away and dining out had pretty much gone by the board although we still occasionally ate in our (cheap) little Greek restaurant.

During this period there was a strange and bizarre incident that to this day I still find almost incredible. The foreman of the builders carrying out the work came into the office one day and gave me a letter in an opened envelope, which he had found lodged behind a doorframe that he had just ripped out in one of the dining rooms. He said that on reading it out of curiosity, the writer had mentioned a couple, Rod and Gill, and so wondered if it referred to us. I saw that the envelope was addressed to my friend Philip (in Nottingham) who had moved down to Eastbourne with me and that the writer was Gill's friend, Deane, who he had married but were now long since divorced. The letter was dated October 1965. I remember Philip returning to Nottingham in the late summer of 1965 and coming down to see Deane in the autumn. The girls (Gill and Deane) had found him accommodation in a guesthouse but if I knew at the time where, I had long since forgotten. For some reason (which I have never found out) he must have re-read it while having breakfast and then stuffed it behind the architrave of the door to the dining room; to be found almost thirty years later when we owned the property!

Our daughter, Karen, who now had two children but was divorced, had started training as a nurse. Our son, Rupert, was now at university but helped out in the hotel during his vacations. Gradually, with the help of the 'new broom' bank manager, we were able to install the new lift into the two-year-old gaping hole next door and thereby were allowed to unlock the interconnecting fire doors and even managed to bring a few extra bedrooms on stream. Each year the turnover increased substantially, although because of the huge interest payments, we only just kept our heads above water.

In October 1993, by selling off some of the old, unwanted furniture in the hotel, we managed to raise sufficient cash to spend three or four days at the Unicorn Hotel in Stow-on-the-Wold, for our twenty-fifth wedding anniversary. The hotel where we had spent our honeymoon, in what were then probably better financial circumstances.

Chapter Eighteen
Friends

Between 1990 and 1995, many of our friends seemed to go through difficult times, not necessarily financial (although sometimes this was the case) but tragic and sometimes, with hindsight, humorous. Four of my close friends and drinking pals, David, Jedd, Rudi and Andy, all died. Two, David and Andy, from cancer, Jedd from a road accident and Rudi (known as the Flying Dutchman) from drink.

Basil (Philip) and Christine who had always had quite a stormy relationship, usually brought about by drink, split up for a time because of Christine's sudden desire to work in Cyprus unaccompanied by Basil. His drinking had become progressively worse and he had managed to crash his car twice. Carless Christine occasionally took a taxi to work and on one of these trips she was told by the Cypriot taxi driver that he could find her a job with his cousin in Cyprus. It was supposed to be managing his restaurant for the summer season but she soon realised it was in fact as a general skivvy, mostly peeling spuds and washing up. She stuck it out for three or four months but as it was difficult to find proper work and the fact that she was working there illegally anyway (Cyprus not being a member of the EU at that time) she decided to return home. In the meantime, Basil had given up his job, or his job had given up Basil, and sold everything they possessed with the 'Sir Galahadian' intention of fetching Christine back. Unfortunately, the good if somewhat optimistic idea went awry and all proceeds from the sale were spent on a two month drinking binge. The furthest he travelled was from their home in Harlow down to Eastbourne, where he stayed with us until Christine returned.

One night, Basil, Oscar and me went out for a drink together and moving on to a jazz club after the pub closed, were propping up the bar when Basil said that he didn't feel well and was going outside for some fresh air. I said I would be out in a couple of minutes as I was ready to leave; and seeing he was 'harpist', told him to wait for me outside and not to wander off. Going upstairs from the cellar bar a couple of minutes later, there was no sign of him. It was only a short walk home so I set off hoping that so long as he had gone in that direction, I would catch him up. Arriving back at the hotel and having seen nothing of Basil, I found two youngsters, about twenty years of age, sitting on the front wall. I asked if they had seen anyone going into the hotel (it was now about one thirty a.m.) they replied that they had just taken a bloke in who had a key but couldn't stand up. They explained that they had just walked down College Road and had heard someone cursing but interspersed with short bursts of song. On investigation they had found two feet protruding from a bush and with a little more rummaging, had found Basil attached to them. With some difficulty, they had hauled him out (Basil was a big bloke) and eventually finding out where he lived, had brought him home. I was very impressed with these two lads, who as it happened were from Wolverhampton, down looking for work in Eastbourne. I offered them twenty pounds for being good Samaritans but although they were obviously short of money, they flatly refused to take anything.

Basil and Christine stayed with us for several months after this, throughout the winter of 1992/3. The strange thing is that although none of us had any money, we all agreed that it was one of the best Christmases that we had ever had.

Alan and Kay had divorced and Alan had met an English girl who lived in Spain. Kay had gone off to live in an Ashram in India and spent a great deal of time meditating and chanting. An amusing little anecdote here is that on one occasion, our friends Graham (Sac) and Ann were flying to India for a holiday and had arranged to travel on the same flight as Kay who was returning to her Ashram. Kay was sitting behind them and they could hear her quiet chant. The flight attendant, who had gathered that the three of them were together, asked Sac what he and Ann would like to drink, and would their friend like something. Sac, placing both forefingers on his temples, closed his eyes and on opening them again said to the hostess, "Nope, she doesn't want anything, thanks."

Ray and Barbara had, in a moment of madness, given up their jobs and decided to go and work for a mutual acquaintance in Cyprus. It only lasted for about eighteen months as once again, this was well before Cyprus became a member of the EU. This meant they were working illegally and so consequently were taken advantage of. When they returned, they managed to get jobs in an hotel in Alfriston and then as managers of a pub/hotel in Rye. But things were never the same between them again.

Ray's drinking became worse and eventually he ran off with the takings from the hotel bar (approximately a thousand pounds) and didn't return until he had spent it all. In the meantime, the Rye police had telephoned me and asked that should he contact me, would I try and encourage him to return to Rye and give himself up. They also mentioned that the company that owned the hotel had said they would not press charges if the money was returned. Sure enough, a few days later I had a call from Ray who said that he had been roaming round East Anglia. I picked him up from the station and explained the position to him. Gill and I scraped together five hundred pounds and I think his mother and aunt raised the other five hundred. I then took him over to Rye, accompanied by Barbara, where we handed him over to the police and he was duly arrested. Barbara and I went off to lunch and returned to the police station at about three p.m. when we had been told that he would be released on bail.

From there on, things went from bad to worse. They found another job in a pub in Mayfield but Ray did the same thing again, disappearing with the takings. This time he was, not unreasonably, threatened with prosecution by the owners or, as an alternative, Barbara would have to work without pay for several months to recompense them. She opted to do this but shortly after finishing her stint and having left and moved back to Eastbourne, she decided that enough was enough and they separated.

However, this wasn't the end of the Ray saga. Sometime in the spring of 1994, I ran into Ray early one morning in town. He looked fairly unkempt, as if he was sleeping rough, although I understood him to be staying with his poor, long-suffering mother. I took him for breakfast to a café that we occasionally used in Seaside Road. I knew that he wasn't working and so asked if he would like a job in the hotel, where he could also live in. I said that with money, decent food and accommodation perhaps he would be able to pull himself together. A forlorn hope, as was subsequently proved. However, for about twelve months he did improve. His drinking didn't actually decrease but with regular meals he appeared to be holding it better. His work was satisfactory and he now kept himself perfectly presentable. There were a number of bizarre episodes (one of which is worth relating) and a few items went missing – nothing of great value – but probably sold to buy more drink.

The incident mentioned above, happened during the winter of 1994/95. It is worth mentioning for two reasons. The first because it has humour but secondly because it shows the tragedy of alcoholism, the gradual destruction of someone's character and mind. The slow erosion and addling of, in this case, an intelligent man's brain. A man who was good company with a quick wit, very good at crosswords, had a greater vocabulary than most and was an excellent artist. Someone who had been capable of holding down senior management positions but had now, more recently, been working as a kitchen porter. During my years in catering, I had met a number of kitchen porters who had in conversation shown themselves to be intelligent people but for one reason or another had dropped through the grid.

All had a drink problem.

I have digressed somewhat, but during February 1995, Gill and I scraped enough money for a week's holiday in Cyprus. We felt reasonably confident in leaving Ray in charge of the closed hotel but on our return we were greeted by an obviously sheepish Ray. He said there had been a break-in and although nothing appeared to have been taken, all the spirits in the drinks cellar had been consumed; presumably by the intruder! On our way down to inspect the cellar, he said that when he went down to see how much was missing (he didn't explain how he knew any was likely to be missing) he had slipped on some water which was leaking from a pipe and had managed to knock twenty or so 'empty scotch and gin (et cetera) bottles onto the concrete floor, so breaking them all.

So far, so implausible.

He produced a stocktake of what the bottles had contained prior to it having been consumed 'by the intruder'. I reminded him that we had jointly carried out a stocktake in January after having been open over the Christmas period and asked why he thought it necessary to do so again. His reply was that he wanted to show that the drink was all there prior to the break-in. I could see there was little point in pursuing this line of enquiry!

To give his story credence, he said that he had called in our builder and our plumber, one to fix the broken window, the other to fix the leak. I spoke to the plumber first, who said that he couldn't find a leak and that it looked as if someone had thrown a bucket of water over the cellar floor. On my speaking to the very amused builder, he told me he had found a mat from the car park entrance hallway, outside the broken window on the car park. It had obviously been used to break the window as it still had glass splinters embedded in it. He had asked Ray how the 'phantom intruder' had gained access to steal the mat from inside the building in order to take it outside and use to break the window glass to gain access back in again.

Are you with me so far?

Poor old Ray could not think of any sensible reason for this. His story was fantastically convoluted and befuddled and with a wonderful lack of logic and distorted chronological order.

Sometime in August 1995, Gill and I took an evening off and went out to have a meal at The Taurus, a steak bar whose Cypriot owner I had known since first coming to Eastbourne. We had left Barbara in charge of the hotel and bar and Ray was there too. Although they were separated, they were still amicable and the plan that night was that when it quietened down in the bar, Ray would go down and cook them a couple of steaks for dinner. At about ten p.m., Nicky (the owner of The Taurus) came to our table and said there was a telephone call for me. It was Barbara to say that Ray had disappeared and had left a fire exit door wide open at the side of the hotel. She was a little concerned at being there alone, particularly as she had no idea how long the security door had been open. We left and returned home. Barbara said that Ray had gone down to the kitchen at about nine thirty p.m. to cook the steak and she had followed some half an hour later. There had been no sign of Ray, or the steaks for that matter, just a number of fire doors thrown open, including the one on the outside.

We saw Ray a few times over the next three or four years, usually in pubs when we were out for a drink with friends. He always looked unkempt and with a heavy drinker's blotchy face.

Soon after he 'ran off', I had a call from him in which he demanded the return of an oven that we had installed in the small flat (bedroom, lounge and bathroom) that we had given him to live in rent free. His muddled brain, for some reason, believed that it belonged to him. For the next few years, until his death in 1999, we had a number of abusive phone calls from him, along with a great number of cards, some vulgar, some threatening, all of which he denied sending in spite of two or three of them being handwritten.

There is no truer saying than 'No good turn ever goes unpunished'.

In the twenty years that the four of us had been friends, we had many happy, fun-filled times together. Holidays abroad, weekends away, dinner parties and barbecues, but none of us could help him.

In 1996, shortly after a holiday with Gill and I in Greece, Barbara met someone else, a far more stable person. They are now married and have a business in Eastbourne.

Chapter Nineteen
Parga

The holiday mentioned (with Barbara) was a week spent in Parga in May 1996, a break for Barbara as Ray was still being a nuisance factor. It was a very enjoyable week for us all, but was particularly memorable for the following story:

We had booked two studio apartments up a steep hill overlooking the harbour. The first night, we went down to the seafront and having looked over a few menus, chose a restaurant called Zorro's. Zorro (his name was actually Angelo) sat us up on a balcony overlooking the sea, saying, "It is a romantic table for a man with two ladies." After a very good meal – there was a lot of Italian influence in Parga, which raises the standard – we carried on drinking and chatting, no doubt to excess! At about eleven p.m. we decided it was time to go and started to climb up the maze of steep narrow passages back to the apartments. On reaching the top, we knew that we had gone too high up but were also confused (read befuddled) to see the sea in front of us, down below. We retraced our steps back down and tried again, this time taking a slightly different route. On reaching the top, there it was again, the sea that we had left behind us now in front of us, down below. By now, our heads starting to clear a little, we realised that we were on a headland, although the realisation of this was still of no help in finding our apartments. Back down we went. It was now after midnight, so it seemed that the sensible thing to do was find a bar and have a coffee and brandy and ask directions. The coffee and brandy were no problem but as the two or three people in the bar spoke no English, directions were more difficult to come by. However, after a few minutes the barman came across to our table and said 'telephone'. Going to the bar with him and picking up the phone, a voice introduced himself as Photas and said that the barman had telephoned him saying that he thought we needed help. I explained the position to him and he said he would come down to see us and hopefully be of some assistance. Ten minutes later, Photas (who spoke good English) appeared and introduced himself. Unfortunately he didn't know our apartments as they were only a small block of some six or eight. However, on my saying that on our arrival that afternoon, we had been deposited by a minibus above them, on what appeared to be the main road, he suggested that the best thing to do was to follow the route. He obviously knew the road I meant because he quickly led us onto it and we started to walk up, looking for and trying to remember which track ran off it to the apartments. It was now about 1.30 am and pitch black. Photas and I were walking a few yards ahead of Gill and Barbara but could still hear them talking behind us. Eventually we reached the top of the hill and I said that we had definitely missed our track as I knew it was not this high up. It was only then that we became aware that Gill and Barbara were no longer behind us. Retracing our steps and calling them, we received no reply. It seemed logical to assume that had they recognised the track down to the apartments, they would have called us; but at the risk of being branded a chauvinist, logic very often appears to be unfamiliar to the female of the species!

I remembered then, but only then, that on our arrival we had left a large container of water on a grass verge at the top of the track, intending to pick it up later. We walked all the way back down the hill but found no sign of the water container and no recognisable track from the numerous tracks that led off the road.

What to do?

Photas was a bit concerned and quite obviously, so was I. They seemed to have just disappeared into the night.

He suggested that we should go to the police station and ask for their assistance. We walked back into the town and found the police station, which was up some stairs over a shop. Photas explained the position to the two officers (one being a sergeant) and after a few questions they agreed to come out and search with us. We all clambered into their Land Rover but it wouldn't start. After several attempts, the sergeant got out and fiddled under the bonnet, which seemed to fix it and off we went. Slowly back up the hill, with the constable leaning out shining a pencil torch into the ditches. It seemed rather churlish to ask why they didn't possess a bigger torch! On the way back down, with the aid of the headlights, I recognised the head of the track down to our apartments. The sergeant stopped the Land Rover and I raced down to check whether or not Gill and Barbara were there. They were, both in their respective beds asleep. Although, of course, I was relieved, at the same time I was furious. I went back up the track to apologise and explain to the police officers and Photas. The sergeant raised his eyebrows and said something in Greek (which sounded rude) then drove off, taking Photas with them.

I went to bed, which fortunately for Gill was a single; otherwise she would probably have received a kick up the backside.

The following morning I was awoken by a hammering and banging on the apartment door, accompanied by Barbara amusingly shouting (or so she thought) "Water. Water. I need water." Not feeling in the least amused, I shouted back a couple of expletives but got up anyway. Letting Barbara in, she went straight to the fridge and took out the container of water that I had last seen at the top of the track. Gill having made coffee and my having calmed down somewhat, the three of us sat down for breakfast, all looking slightly the worse for wear. I asked what had happened but with little confidence that I was to receive a sensible or logical explanation. The girls said they had spotted the water container and had therefore known they had found the right track down to the apartments. There appeared to be no sensible reason as to why, on finding the track, they hadn't called us, knowing we were only a few yards ahead. Furthermore, apart from the fact that they may have been thirsty in the night, there appeared to be no logic attached to their taking in the water container and so removing any clue for us, when we inevitably retraced our steps.

I gave up. I know when I am beaten.

A man may as well concede an argument when his wife gives him the look which says, 'Why don't you understand my explanation, are you mad or just stupid'. When her friend gives you the same look, at the same time, then you know you have lost!

Later that morning, I went down into town and bought two bottles of scotch. I took one up to Photas at his hotel and thanked him for his help. The other I took to the police station later in the day. The sergeant had regained his sense of humour and greeting me like an old friend, insisted that we had a drink together.

Chapter Twenty
1995

We had finally got a court date, late September 1995. In about March of that year, Malcolm (our solicitor) had a letter from the accountants' insurer's solicitors, with an offer of forty thousand pounds in full and final settlement of our claim. It was obvious that this paltry figure was a 'fishing expedition' but of course the important point was that they had accepted liability. I instructed Malcolm to write back as dismissively as only solicitors can (I am sure the ability to do this is enshrined in their Articles). I knew that we would almost certainly have to make an application for bankruptcy in the winter of 95/96, or sooner if the court case went against us; but of course they didn't know this.

In about May, we had a further offer of a hundred and fifty thousand. We agreed that this should be turned down with equal disdain. Malcolm was a little concerned at our refusing the figure, pointing out that if we went to court, it was possible (if unlikely) that we may be awarded a lower figure. However, the facts were that we had a rough estimate of Legal Aid costs which would have to be repaid, approximately fifty thousand pounds. The bank borrowing now stood at a fairly hefty three hundred thousand and the hotel was probably only valued at about the same figure.

We had a new bank manager, our wonderful, helpful 'new broom' had moved on. I didn't trust the new guy, there was something about him and eventually I was proved correct in my suspicions. It seemed to me if we accepted one hundred and fifty thousand, settled the Legal Aid bill, so leaving a hundred thousand, the bank would definitely want this. It would mean that we would not have the means to complete the hotel, which I estimated at between one hundred thousand and one hundred and fifty thousand pounds; and therefore not be in the position to increase the turnover, which in turn meant no increase in valuation. Without being able to do this, our over-friendly bank manager might very well decide that as the bank was still owed two hundred thousand and the hotel would probably fetch three hundred thousand, it might be a good idea to force a sale.

When I was in my twenties, I used to play poker regularly on a Friday night. I now found that in spite of what was at stake, I was getting a similar adrenalin rush. Rather like a feeling of confidence one sometimes gets when playing cards, I felt we could push the insurers a lot further. Of course, sometimes you are wrong!

We heard nothing until late August and then Malcolm received a very strange letter which inter alia said, 'We have offered your clients compensation of one hundred and fifty thousand pounds against their claim, are we still a long way apart?' I suggested to Malcolm that his reply should be just one word, 'yes'. He embellished it a little but in essence that is what he said. This time we only had to wait until the first week of September, when an offer of three hundred and sixty thousand was received. Although this perhaps did not quite put us back in the position that we were in four years earlier, it was near enough and we accepted it.

The net settlement of three hundred and ten thousand (after repaying the Legal Aid fund) arrived in our bank account in September. As I had anticipated, our over-friendly bank manager asked if we would clear the overdraft completely. Oscar wanted to draw thirty-five thousand to purchase another leasehold pub and as my estimate to complete the necessary works was up to one hundred and fifty thousand, I said that I would only pay the residue off the overdraft. I pointed out to him that this would not only reduce the borrowing substantially but would, within a couple of years, enable us to double the turnover by bringing all the bedrooms on stream. He assured me that if the borrowing was cleared, there would be no problems in raising the necessary funds to finish it off. I didn't trust him but agreed to pay a further fifty thousand in any event. Needless to say, when I applied for more funding he told me they would require a new valuation at a cost of some three thousand to us. I was very annoyed, being exactly what I expected seemed to make it worse, so I decided to ignore him and go over his head. I wrote a long letter to the CEO at NatWest, setting out the problems that we had experienced over the past few years, pointing out the help we had received from the previous manager and the hindrance that we were receiving at present. In good faith we had reduced the borrowing further than I had wished because we had been assured that further funding would be no problem and that I certainly saw a further three thousand pounds for a valuation as a problem. I received an acknowledgement and things happened very quickly. We were told that a valuation was unnecessary, or if it was, it would be paid for by the bank and that the extra funding was now available.

Although it had been trying, draining and hard work for four years, it had provided us with one huge advantage over nearly all the other hotels in Eastbourne.

Our original intention was to turn it into a coaching hotel, as this was the only way that any hotel in Eastbourne (of sufficient size to take a coach) could survive. But because we had never had sufficient bedrooms in operation to take a full coach, we were only ever able to take private guests. There was a huge difference in tariff rates, at least two or three times as much. We were eventually able to command more per room for three nights' accommodation than a coach company would pay for a week. Neither did we have the expense and nuisance factor of entertainment, which was an integral part of the coach contract.

Chapter Twenty-One
Oscar

During the years 1992-1995 that we were fighting the negligence/breach of contract action, our relationship with Oscar, who until then I had probably considered my closest friend, gradually deteriorated.

The original partnership agreement was to have been on a fifty-fifty basis, with Gill and I investing a hundred and fifty thousand pounds and Alan doing the same, but in two tranches – fifty thousand to start and another one hundred thousand when he had sold his business, a pub in Bramber. On the expected return of the forty thousand capital gains tax, this was going to be a loan from us but of course it never materialised. Gill and I were to run the hotel with Alan being a silent partner. However, a few months into when the problems arose with the capital gains tax, he tried to pull out of the agreement, even though, as I pointed out to him, this would almost certainly push us into bankruptcy. The terms of the partnership in regard to a sale were standard, that should any party wish to sell their share, then a valuation would be necessary. I had to agree to his request but I knew that because of the drop in the value of property in general, the value would probably be half the valuation of some two years previously when we had purchased the freehold. Oscar had not at that point sold his business and had only in fact put in forty thousand. When the valuation was prepared and the various adjustments made, not only would his share be of no value but in fact he would owe us about five thousand. He changed his mind but I never trusted him again. Eventually the pub was sold and the rest of the investment came in.

We had numerous meetings, which gradually became more infrequent. Early on I said to him that although the original agreement made him a silent partner, things had changed so drastically that the partnership agreement needed adjustment. Gill and I were entitled to a salary of twenty-five thousand per annum, but although working eighteen hours per day we were drawing virtually nothing. I suggested that as he and Linda were doing nothing at present and I was aware that they were short of money too, the answer would be for them to work with us in the hotel. This would cut down on staff, we would waive our entitlement to the twenty-five thousand salary and merely split the profit two ways. He wasn't interested. He said that he wanted to purchase a leasehold pub as he was in line to be chairman of the local Licensed Victuallers Association (LVA) the following year.

Being chairman of the LVA is apparently a very expensive business. But although Oscar was in a precarious financial position, he was determined to have his twelve months in the limelight. The position is very often held by self-opinionated, boastful individuals, although not always, who always carry a wad of at least five hundred pounds in their back pocket. This very often being produced with a flourish to buy a round, usually accompanied by the comment, 'The lunchtime takings'.

The phrase Publicanis Vulgaris seemed to be an apt description of some of his cohorts at that time. It was a little like a chicken and egg situation. I was never quite sure whether you became like that when you became a publican or whether it was necessary as a prerequisite to becoming one!

Within the partnership agreement there was a clause which Alan appeared to be unaware of. This stated that if we were unable to draw our twenty-five thousand salary (or any part of it) it would be treated as an ongoing loan from us and subject to five per cent annual interest rate. As he had turned down my suggestions of a way round our problems, I said that this clause would now be implemented. The effect of this meant that over time Oscar's share would be reduced, by virtue of the business owing us an increasing amount of money.

He always appeared to blame us for the predicament we had found ourselves in, although he knew that the problems arose from the negligence of the accountant. Bizarrely, although we were suing that firm jointly as a partnership, Oscar continued to use him in a private capacity and in fact in his new pub when he eventually purchased one.

Over the next few years, we gradually bought extra percentages of Oscar's share in order to fund his lifestyle. This continued to the extent that along with the thirty-five thousand pounds that he had drawn to purchase his new pub, by 1997/98 we had bought his share completely.

This wasn't quite the end of our connection though! In 1998/99, he instructed a firm of solicitors from Brighton to bring an action against us for breach of contract, and at the same time insinuated that we had drawn more from the business than our entitlement. This went no further than my writing back to the firm setting out the facts and enclosing copies of the various partnership agreements, five I think, in total. I knew that his solicitors would not have had the benefit of seeing these as Oscar would not have been in possession of all of them, if any. He didn't believe in paperwork! I heard nothing further so guessed that my assumption was correct. We saw little of him in subsequent years, but heard that he had moved with Linda, to live in Spain and had sadly died in 2011.

Chapter Twenty-Two
October 1995-2001

The settlement was definitely a cause for celebration, the telephone call coming on my fiftieth birthday. Gill had already arranged a surprise dinner with a number of our friends in our favourite restaurant and much to their delight, we were able to pay for all, as they had expected to have to cough up.

Once all the work was completed, which stretched out over the winter and spring of 96/97 and then on into 97/98, we started to make the profits that we should have been making from the beginning. We were able to employ more staff and although Rupert did work for us whilst at university, on finishing in 1996, he decided it wasn't for him.

We had a number of holidays in the autumn and spring of 95/96. Sorrento for a week, the week in Parga with Barbara and as Rupert was attending Limoges University during the winter and spring of 95/96 we spent some time there and in Bordeaux.

During October of 1996, we also decided to take a driving holiday abroad, the first since our ill-fated trip in 1989. Our intention was to drive down through France, Switzerland and Italy and take the ferry from Ancona to Igoumenitsa in Greece, a trip that we have done many times since. A place that we definitely wanted to visit was a village named Lia in the Morgana Mountains in northern Greece, almost on the Albanian border.

Sometime early in the summer, Rupert had picked up a book in a second-hand book shop, entitled *Eleni*. It was written by a Greek, Nicholas Gage, who now lived in America but covered his young and tragic life up to about nine years of age. It compares the terror of invasion (1940) first by the Italians and then by the Germans, against the quiet, pastoral life in his tiny village. It goes on to show that sometimes civil war (1947) can be more brutal than invasion by a foreign power. It relates that during the two or three years of civil war, his family was starved, beaten and imprisoned in the cellar of their own home by fellow Greeks – communists. How some of his siblings were abducted and marched into captivity in Albania and finally, how his mother (Eleni), along with some of the other villagers, was taken into a ravine and executed. He and two of his sisters managed to escape and eventually made their way to America, where they joined their father, who had been living there since before the War. Nicholas Gage became an investigative journalist on (I think) the *Wall Street Journal* and *New York Times*. A film was made of his book sometime in the 1980s.

Rupert, having read the book before me, said that he would like to join us on the trip. We stayed in Lia for about four nights in a guesthouse built and owned by Nicholas Gage. The single lady (Dina) who ran it for him, although being quite a good cook, produced three different pork dinners the first three nights of our stay. As we were the only people there, we determined to have a change, so drove down to Filiates, the nearest small town, and procured a chicken.

The problem now was to try to explain to Dina what we wanted as she spoke no English. On our return I did my best and she carried it away with what Rupert pessimistically described as an 'air of triumph', also adding that he felt it unlikely that we would see it again! However, on coming down to dinner at about seven p.m., we were greeted by a lovely aroma and two friends of Dina's, the lady being able to speak English. She told us that Dina had telephoned in some confusion as to whether the chicken was a present for her or to be cooked for us. But much to Rupert's relief, the chicken was now in the oven, with onions and potatoes and would be ready for us soon.

The couple, Angelo and Maria, were friends of Nick Gage and had lived in America for several years. Maria spoke fluent American with a strong Bronx accent but Angelo spoke no English at all. The next day they showed us round the village, including many of the places mentioned in the book. They also showed us the house and cellar, now a ruin, where the family had been imprisoned.

When we left Lia, we again boarded a ferry from Igoumenitsa, but this time to Corfu to take Rupert to the airport to catch a plane home. We returned to the Greek mainland and continued our holiday.

Some years later, I think about 2005, we were once again in Lia and met Nick Gage's wife and daughter. They showed us over what was, by then, the rebuilt family home.

November 1996

On our return from Greece, towards the end of November, Rupert told us that he was moving to Nottingham in January of the following year. He felt, and he was quite right, that with a decent degree there were few prospects for him in Eastbourne. His decision to move to Nottingham appeared to be based on the fact that I had lived there as a young man.

Chapter Twenty-Three

With Rupert and Karen definitely not interested in coming into the business with us, we decided that for the 1998 season we needed to bite the bullet and employ some permanent staff, even though we usually closed for four months during the winter. By offering much higher salaries and the attraction of longer holidays than the norm, we managed to find an excellent, conscientious young chef, an assistant manager, a housekeeper and a somewhat tipsy but efficient and engaging barman. Around these 'heads of departments' we built a good nucleus of full time and temporary staff. This made life much easier for us and we were able to take the occasional couple of days' break away from the business during the summer months. Something hitherto unknown.

The main problem that we experienced with staff were the people we employed to service the bedrooms and to serve in the dining rooms. These were usually young and nearly all girls. We had managed to replicate the trio (plus one) of girls that had worked for us at The Park View. This new quadrille (in the sense of a troupe), Benita, Anita, Lisa and Cheryl, all started with us when they were quite young (fourteen to fifteen years of age) and continued through their university years. They all worked hard and were totally reliable and when they were a little older and had got over their teenage angst – great company, Benita, the first of the foursome to start with us, became like a surrogate daughter. She only ever seemed to eat chocolate and sausages and could be very amusing, although she didn't mean to be. In her teenage years she possessed the same gangly awkwardness that The Dragon had been blessed with and on one occasion somehow managed to pour a basin full of duck fat over her head.

However, when we finally had thirty bedrooms in operation, we needed extra staff. The problems arose when we started to employ girls of school leaving age (plus) on a full-time basis. They were nearly all unreliable, especially on a Saturday morning when they had been out the night before. The fact that we paid a much higher rate than all the other hotels appeared to make no difference whatsoever, they were just not conscientious. Our salvation came in 97/98 when we were contacted by a foreign student language school in Eastbourne, when we were asked if we could employ any of their students. These were usually all girls of university age and of various nationalities who came to learn English for three or six months at a time. The only drawback was that we had to provide accommodation. We very quickly found a couple of small flats in a modern block for sale, and in buying these our staff problems were over. The girls were from all over Europe but predominantly from Spain and Holland. They worked hard, were always punctual and didn't go out and get drunk! In fact, many of them commented on the amount that English youngsters consumed and really couldn't understand why.

With our enthusiastic chef Keith, and Hugh our assistant manager, heading a team of fifteen to twenty, the last three or four years were a smooth and enjoyable operation.

With hindsight we have often asked ourselves why we sold!

The name Devonshire Park Hotel was suggested by our son, Rupert, early in 1992, to replace the two original guesthouses, Medwyn and Silverford. It was probably the first new hotel to be opened in Eastbourne since the War, with the exception of the TGW building on the seafront.

After years of trials and tribulation it eventually became our most successful business.

We sold the hotel in November 2001. Initially, we bought a rather nice penthouse apartment at the top of Meads, Eastbourne. Although it had splendid views over that area and out to sea, we soon realised it was not quite what we wanted. We travelled extensively in Europe over the next few years, moving our home (our base) from Eastbourne to Shropshire, then to Spain and back to Shropshire, before settling (so far) where we are now.

Karen, our daughter, has remarried and is happy in her career as a nurse in the General Hospital, Eastbourne. She has two grown up children from her first marriage, Paul and Sarah. Rupert, our son, is an executive in an American bank based in Nottingham. He and his partner, Kelly, have two children, Molly and Maisy.

Gill and I now live in a seventeenth-century cottage with an acre of garden, in Herefordshire. It is on the border with Wales where we walk in the hills two or three times a week.

When the hotel was sold in 2001, I was fifty-six and Gill fifty-four, so our intention was always to buy another business. Somehow or another, we still, at the time of writing (2015) have not got round to it.

Epilogue

I was prompted into writing this short autobiography (if that is not too grand a title) for two reasons. The first being that it might provide some interest (or boredom) to future generations of our family; however, the second is because in the last few years, 2008–2015, an insidious enmity has developed, whereby our generation, the so-call Baby Boomers, are being criticised for what has become a perceived opinion that we have had it too good!   The main proponents advocating this theory are employees of the BBC and a few politicians.

(Please see Britain's Inequalities)

What I am going to say next is not in any way meant to be boastful, quite the opposite in fact, because as previously mentioned, with more single-mindedness we could, without doubt, have been financially better off than we are! It is merely to illustrate what can be done with youth, determination, a willingness to work and an acceptance that if you want to succeed, it is almost certainly down to one's self.
When I arrived in Eastbourne on April 12th 1965, I had about forty pounds and all my possessions fitted into one suitcase (I also had my lunch in a knotted handkerchief suspended from a stick, but no cat!). When we sold the hotel and other properties in 2001 (age fifty-six) we had sufficient to retire.
    If this sounds smug and it certainly isn't meant to be, as it could hardly be described as an entrepreneurial legend of our time, it is just to emphasise the fact that it could be done then and I am sure it is still possible now.
    I appreciate that property prices in comparison to average salaries (especially in London and the south east) are much higher than say the 1960s and 70s. During this time, when we lived in Eastbourne, a two or three bedroomed terraced property would have been nine to eleven thousand pounds. With an average salary of perhaps seventeen hundred to two thousand pounds per annum, this would have meant a ratio of some five to six times salary. Now I see the same properties are selling for one hundred and seventy thousand with a supposed

average salary of twenty-five thousand per annum (although I think it less in Eastbourne), some seven times salary. So looking at property values, the gap seems immense, but looking at average salaries and the lowest mortgage rates ever, then perhaps the gap is not quite so huge. However, I do concede that it is a problem but I am not sure how it is the fault of the older generation.

I genuinely believe that part of the problem is the 'want it now and will have it now' society that we live in. The culture where youngsters appear to believe that fulfilment lies only in fame, perhaps as a footballer or successful contestant on a TV talent show. These can of course be gateways to success, but only for the very (talented) few. I am afraid that the other ninety-nine per cent of us have to make our own way by our own volition and with what little talent we possess.

I had mentioned earlier that we were the 'lucky generation' but this was as compared to our parents and grandparents who suffered wars and real austerity and deprivation. But we were willing to work hard and put in long hours to achieve what we wanted. Having bought our first business (a mistake) in 1968, six years later we were still running round in a fifty-pound second-hand car and sleeping in what was, to all intents and purposes, a shed! The big cars and exotic holidays did not come until much later.

Finally though, there is one thing I do concede and that is not everyone will be fortunate enough to find a Gill!

A Tour Through Europe

In October 2002 we arranged a holiday in Cyprus with six of our friends, in a rented villa in Paphos. Earlier, in September, my sister, Marylyn and Martin had booked a holiday in Thasos, so we decided to go by car, linking the two together. Our intention was to spend a week or so on the Greek mainland before arriving in Thasos, spend time there and then drive to Piraeus to catch a ferry to Cyprus.

We had travelled on this ferry (which was a two-day journey) a couple of years before. We had not been impressed with the food (to put it mildly) but had enjoyed the journey, so thought it would be nice to do it again. On that trip, on going down to dinner the first night, the choice on the menu was pork chop and chips, or chips and pork chop. Having had a surfeit of chips over the previous weeks, we asked our waiter, who looked about a hundred and ten, if we could have some other form of potato rather than chips. He didn't understand me, or didn't want to, so when our main course chops arrived, they were accompanied by the ubiquitous chips, which he proceeded to serve. At an adjacent table, I could see what looked like a dish of small new potatoes. I asked the waiter to stop serving us chips and bring us some potatoes, pointing at the other table but he just carried on anyway. A very smartly dressed Greek man got up from, what now seemed in my mind, a table receiving preferential treatment, and came across and asked if he could be of any assistance. I explained the problem, to which he chuckled and said they weren't potatoes but the most disgusting frozen sprouts cooked until they were white, but we were welcome to some if we wished. I thanked him but declined and we resigned ourselves to what was on out plates.

On boarding the ferry, we had got chatting to a young Israeli couple and a Romanian engineer. The ferry eventually went on from Limassol to Haifa. They had travelled on this boat on a previous occasion and had warned us about the standard of food; having come prepared themselves. Dan, the Romanian, said that the next day we docked at Rhodes for a couple of hours and that there was a good restaurant near the quay. We took advantage of this and had a very good lunch.

August 2002

Towards the end of August, we set off by ferry from Newhaven to Dieppe and stayed the first night at an Ibis hotel in Chateau Thierry. The next day we continued as far as La Bresse in the Vosges mountains, intending to stay at the Ibis there but found that it wasn't built yet. However, we found a small Auberge (Le Couchetat) and staying a couple of nights, had two excellent meals – Touffaye and Beckoffe – the whole thing, including drinks, coming to two hundred and three euros. This, when the euro was worth about sixty-three pence.

Switzerland

Leaving the Vosges mountains, we drove into Switzerland heading for a small, family hotel where we had stayed on a number of occasions. This was situated on the side of Lake Lucerne at Gersau, and was owned and run by a Swiss chef and his wife, he having trained at The Ritz in London. The food was always first class and after finishing in the kitchen, he would come out and play a barrel organ in the restaurant. His wife was always pregnant and from a standing start, had four or possibly five children in quick succession. Every year we would receive a Christmas card with a photograph of the family, including the latest arrival.

We always had the same room, which was a lovely suite with a balcony overhanging the lake itself. The first time that we stayed there, we were unaware that there was a berth for one of the lake's steamboats immediately to the left of our balcony. One evening, after indulging in some pre-dinner hanky-panky, to work up an appetite, we were laying starkers on the giant bed, when a steamboat hove into view, not ten yards from our window. It was too late! There must have been fifty people on the two decks, laughing and waving at us. We just hoped none of them were staying at the hotel.

We spent two or three days walking on Rigi (the local mountain) and took a boat trip (from our balcony) to Lucerne. There are a number of ways to access the top of Rigi, by train from Vitnau, by a large cable car from Weggis and several two-seater cable cars from various other points. Franz, the chef/patron, was always happy to come and pick us up from wherever we came off the mountain. He had a lovely, and beautifully kept, old Packard that he had bought in London and brought back to Switzerland. On one of our walks, we were looking out for a mountain restaurant that he had told us about and spotted a number of people in the distance, standing drinking outside a chalet. When we approached and entered through a small wicket gate, we saw that there was a large barbecue in operation with a chef cooking chicken, steaks and sausages. Walking up to it, we began discussing what we would eat when the chef, speaking perfect English, informed us that it was a private house and not a restaurant! However, he did point the restaurant out to us, which was only some half mile away.

Leaving Lake Lucerne and eventually taking the motorway through the Gotthard Tunnel, we decided to spend a couple of days by Lake Garda. We had been before and have been again since, always staying on the western shore as it is quieter and less commercialised.

Italy

On our last visit, we had lunch in a small restaurant in a village called Campione. The tunnels on the western side of the lake are horrendous, narrow and badly lit, and with a mad right fork within one of them which takes one down to Campione. Arriving without mishap, we found the restaurant in the main square and remembering they had rooms to let, booked in. Tonino, the chef/patron, only had two letting room with a shared loo and shower. The shower appeared to be a Belfast type sink that one had to clamber into but as the other room wasn't occupied, it was not a problem. The cost being forty euros a night, which included a very good breakfast of cold meat and eggs, there was no room for complaint.

That evening, we had a wonderful meal of carpaccio of beef to start and one of the best lasagnes ever. The fillet was rolled in oil and chopped basil and Tonino said that he left it to marinate, usually overnight. Other meals that we had were, veal and mushrooms, risottos and particularly good veal chops.

We spent three days in Campione, one day longer than intended as the food was quite exceptional. Our time there was only marred by being given a parking ticket (forty euros) for parking in the square and although the police officer apologised profusely, somehow it didn't make me feel any better. However, he did direct us to some parking which was in what appeared to be a giant warehouse, now devoid of whatever, no longer extant, industry that they were built for.

Campione has a very nice, small beach, from where one can take a strenuous walk up the cliffs to Piccata and Tremasine, about two hours.

On the two other occasions that we have visited Lake Garda, we have stayed at the Hotel Olivi, high above the south-western shore; and Hotel Forbsicle, which is in the most beautiful position, directly on the side of the lake. Both hotels serve very good food (although not quite to the standard of Tonino's) with Hotel Olivi being the better of the two but Forbsicle making up for it in entertainment value. Forbsicle was run by a family of four, Angelo and his wife, Grizzela, who were probably in their late sixties, and their two children, Stefano and Vittoria, who were about thirty. Stefano and Vittoria were always arguing and in fact, while we were there, on one occasion Vittoria left and stayed away for two days. Stefano complained bitterly, to anyone who would listen, how irresponsible his sister was and how much extra work it meant for him. I suggested to him that anyone as beautiful as Vittoria could easily be forgiven. Being a temperamental Italian, he said that I was mad and obviously needed glasses! He did come and apologise later, although I had found it amusing.

There was a dance organised for the guests every Thursday evening, on a terrace overlooking the lake. Angelo said that this was to celebrate fifty years in the hotel but also said, with a twinkle in his eye, "It is good for me to dance with the ladies, it keeps me young."

Grizzela, who did the cooking, just wanted to retire. A couple of guests who we had been chatting to had mentioned that we were retired hoteliers. Thereafter, whenever Grizzela spotted us, she would harangue Angelo with the cry, "Why we no retiro?"

Leaving Campione, we caught the ferry across to Malcesine from Limone and then turning south and bypassing Verona, we picked up the A22 down to Modena.

In 1996 when we had travelled this route with Rupert, it had 'sheeted' down with rain virtually all the way from north of Milano and was still raining when we reached Modena. In desperation, we stopped at a fairly scruffy looking motel. We had to share a room as there was only one available and there was no restaurant. Having our usual basic stores, bread, wine and a bottle of Scotch, Rupert volunteered to go out and try to find something to supplement these victuals. He returned about an hour later with a huge pile of tomato sandwiches. He had tried to buy some salads and meats at a delicatessen, but something being lost in translation, he ended up with only the pile of sandwiches that the woman had insisted on making for him. On the way back, he was chatted up by two Italian girls who invited him to a party, so I suppose we were lucky to get anything at all.

The room had three beds, a table and three chairs so we were able to eat in relative comfort. Gill chose the middle bed and Rupert and I, having sat up late drinking whisky, kept her awake most of the night by snoring in unison on either side.

The next day the weather had cleared and we drove down to Ancona, booking into a small hotel by the docks, called Gino's. Although the hotel itself was very downmarket, the restaurant, which was open to the general public, was excellent. The following day we caught a ferry to Igoumenitsa.

Returning now to our journey 2002, Gill and I on arriving in Modena, found rather better accommodation at the Hotel Eden. One of the reception staff said there was a very good pizzeria at the rear of the hotel, which traded under the unlikely name of Nelson's. Here and on subsequent occasions we have eaten some very good meals. The pizzas, which are cooked in the ovens in front of you, are thin and crispy with whatever topping one chooses.

Arriving in Ancona, we stayed at The Jolly Hotel, which is high up overlooking the town.

Next day we went down to the docks to book a ferry and found there was an Anek Line sailing at four p.m. We reserved a first class cabin, although not one of the most expensive luxury cabins. Having boarded and then going up to the reception desk, we were greeted by the fat purser who was allocating cabins. For some reason he remembered us from the couple of times that we had sailed with them before and, greeting us like old friends, immediately upgraded us to a luxury cabin.

We had a passable dinner although Strinitz Lines serves better food, and having slept well, arrived in Igoumenitsa about eleven a.m.; having called in at Corfu first. Disembarking, we found the little tavern by the docks that we had used on previous visits and ate fried eggs and grilled Serrano, or at least the Greek version.

The big ferries, in those days, used to dock immediately on the seafront, but have now been moved out of the town to new docks and a reception building that resembles an airport.

Greece

That night we stayed at The Aktion Hotel, which is right on the seafront and family run. We had a room with a balcony overlooking the docks and ate at a small tavern round the corner.

The washbasin in the bathroom didn't have a plug, so I went down and found George (the owner) who appeared to be quite barmy and certainly, from a photograph of him in his younger days, looked quite Teutonic. I asked if he had any spare sink plugs, his reply was why did I want a spare one, why did I need two? I explained that I didn't want two, I hadn't got one at all and wondered, therefore, if he had any spares. He muttered something about guests stealing his plugs, so slightly irritated but more amused, I asked if that would be the originals or the spares. He ignored me but, opening up his safe, peered in (somewhat optimistically I thought) and then turning round said with a note of satisfaction, that there were no spare plugs.

I gave up but we always carried a spare plug thereafter.

We have stayed at The Aktion quite a few times since and eventually George grows on you, his wife and daughter are lovely people.

Off to Sagiada

Sagiada is a village on the north-west coast of Greece, only a couple of miles or so from the Albanian border. It has a very small quay which has about three or four tavernas, the first of these serving the best fried prawns that I have ever eaten. Although we had been before, we had never stayed, it being only about an hour and a half from Lia, so this time we decided to spend a couple of nights there. There were no obvious hotels or guesthouses but prior to our lunch, we had seen a sign on a telegraph pole that said accommodation, along with a telephone number. After our prawns we telephoned the number and very quickly a taxi appeared, the driver of which was also the owner of the guesthouse. We followed him back and he showed us a large, well-furnished apartment, at twenty-five euros a night. We spent an enjoyable couple of days there, eating a lot more prawns, before driving up for a few days in Lia.

It seems that every time we go to Lia, there is someone new managing the guesthouse and on this visit it was a couple from Athens. I assumed that it is never particularly busy as certainly most times we have stayed, we were the only guests. The book and film (set in this village) is probably long forgotten and Lia, if nothing else, is a long way off the beaten track.

We were threatened with goat stew for dinner and when it finally arrived at about 10.30 pm, it was very good. In the meantime we had chatted to the husband while his wife was cooking. He had lit a fire and was playing a tape of the soundtrack of *Zorba the Greek*. Subsequently we searched all over Greece and Cyprus for a copy of this and eventually found one in a small supermarket in Paphos.

On our first full day in Lia, we went for a long walk high up into the mountains. We first walked along the road, back through Vavouri and up to the even more isolated village of Tsamontas, which is tucked in a ravine within two or three kilometres of the Albanian border. We saw no one in Tsamontas and in fact it had the appearance of being uninhabited, although we knew that it wasn't. We then started to climb, heading in an eastward direction, knowing that the border dropped southwards at one point, bringing it within a kilometre or so of the road below us. We cut across the southern flank of the highest mountain, at 1800 metres, the northern flank of which drops down into Albania.

After lunch, we headed in a south-easterly direction to bring us above Lia. Scrambling down a quite steep stretch, we saw a dusty track below us, which we headed for, seeing that it went in the direction we wanted to take. We started off along the track but within a couple of hundred yards it swung round a sharp bend and we came face to face with a soldier pointing a rifle at us. He said something to us in what we hoped was Greek and not Albanian! Although I was pretty certain of our position, it is always a little difficult in the wilder mountainous areas of Europe, without the aid of large scale maps. This was before GPS and our walk had been done with a compass and a form of dead reckoning. In any event, I replied in English, speaking neither Greek nor Albanian, and said that we were British. He looked uncomprehending but fortunately an officer came out of the building to one side of the track and he was able to converse with us. He seemed to know that we were staying in Lia, which has very few visitors, and explained to us that this was a Greek border post and although the border was a couple of kilometres further on, anyone coming from that direction was assumed to be Albanian. Without further problems, we made our way down to Lia.

Two or three days later, we set off south towards Parga and at lunchtime found ourselves in a small village called Gliki, which is situated on a wide river. We had a very good lunch of local fresh trout in a tavern on one side of the river and then made our way to Parga. Being September, Parga was too busy for us, so staying only one night, we set off the next morning for the Pindos Mountains in north-central Greece.

That night, after walking during the day in these mountains, which are situated north-east of Ioannina, we misjudged our time and arrived back at the car park just as dusk was falling. Knowing that we were a long way from the nearest village that was likely to have accommodation, we decided to spend the night in the Landcruiser. We always carried something to eat, plus wine, tea, coffee, bread and eggs, and a small stove, so it was not a problem. After spending a reasonably comfortable night, we were awake early and, looking at the map, saw that if we drove back down the mountain for about a mile, we would be able to watch the sun rise and probably cook breakfast there. We set off but within a quarter of a mile we were suddenly attacked by a pack of six or seven huge mountain dogs. They jumped at the doors, two were on the bonnet and even one we heard on the roof. I put my foot down on the accelerator and they flew off in all directions. We went a little further down and having watched the sun rise, decided that it may be imprudent to start frying bacon as we weren't very far from where we had met the dogs and of course, they may have decided to join us for breakfast!

To continue our journey, we had to return the same way and on reaching the spot that we had seen the dogs, there was no sign of them, I stopped. I cautiously got out of the car and walking to the edge of the road, I could see for miles down the mountain. In the distance, several hundred feet below where I stood, I could see the dogs trotting in single file downhill, for all the world like a line of soldiers.

We continued on for a few miles eventually reaching a metalled road. Very soon we came across a transport café completely on its own and at the top of the pass. We had a strange but appetising breakfast and some excellent coffee. The young waitress spoke a little English so I asked about the dogs. She said they were probably shepherds' dogs but very often ran as a pack and could be vicious.

Apart from Gill and I, there was only one other customer so I asked the girl if they were ever busy in such an isolated spot. She explained that it was a route used by lorry drivers from Igoumenitsa, through Grevena and into Bulgaria and as it was still very early (six a.m.) there were several drivers still asleep in their wagons at the rear of the café.

Having told her we had slept in the car, she said there were showers downstairs for the use of customers and we were welcome to use them if we wished.

After a shower and feeling refreshed, we decided to stay in the Pindos Mountains for a further day, before going north-west to Papingo and the Vikos Gorge and then joining the northern road which went east to Thessalonika.

After the excitement of the dogs and just before we came across the café, we had seen a sign pointing up another road, which said 'Refuge', at so many kilometres. We thought we would try our luck there that night but arrive in plenty of time to be able to return to the transport café if we couldn't get in, or it didn't exist!

We eventually arrived at the refuge at about four p.m. but on enquiring about staying the night, the girl we spoke to said they had accommodation but they were single sex dormitories, a bit like a youth hostel. However, whilst talking to her the owner turned up and said that as they weren't busy, we were welcome to a dormitory for our sole use. Our dormitory consisted of about ten double bunk beds.

When we went down for dinner, we had one of the best meals we had ever eaten in Greece. There was a choice of two or three dishes both for first and main courses. I can't remember the first course but we both had a delicious casserole as a main. There only appeared to be three other guests, two men and a girl, probably in their thirties. We got chatting to the owner who spoke fairly good English. He asked if we had seen any of the ancient bridges and on our saying no, he went off and came back with a book that contained photographs of perhaps about twenty. They were beautiful old packhorse bridges, high-arched and only of sufficient width for two people to walk over side by side, and some even narrower than that. He said that they were a feature of the Pindos and pointed out several on the map, in a cluster south-west of Grevena. He gave us the map and although it was printed in Greek, we were able to pinpoint the bridges on our own map, the next day.

The following morning before breakfast, Gill managed one of her eccentric interludes. She went off downstairs to the communal shower rooms and on her return, with just a towel wrapped round her, went into the wrong dormitory. Mistaking a form in a bunk (covered in a blanket) over in the corner, for me, she went over and shook it, saying something like, come on, stop messing about, it's time you were up. A young, bearded face appeared from under the blanket, looking terrified and shouting something in Greek. The noise woke up the other occupant of the room, who sat up with a start too. Gill raced for the door like something deranged but, unfortunately, losing her towel, she exited the room stark naked. On her eventually finding our dormitory, I was still asleep so didn't notice her lack of apparel.

While we were having breakfast, the three young people we had seen the night before came down for theirs. The two young men shouted good morning to us and waved, the three of them grinning like Cheshire cats. I remarked to Gill that they seemed particularly friendly this morning, bearing in mind they had not spoken to us the night before. She explained why!

The following night we stayed in Papingo near the Vikos Gorge, in a small government guesthouse. It was run by a young couple and a visiting friend. We had a very nice dinner, what appears to be the Greek national dish, or at least in rural areas, of chicken, potatoes and onions cooked slowly in the oven with oil and thyme. Delicious. The meal was accompanied by some local red wine, quite palatable, but very heavy and therefore a little on the sweet side for our taste.

We were given a room which overlooked the mountains and faced the cliffs of the Vikos, not too far away. There was a huge balcony, bigger than the room itself, probably the roof of a room underneath.

After dinner we had a drink with the trio but only one of the lads spoke a little English. So going up to our room we sat on the balcony for an hour or so drinking a bottle of our own wine which was much more to our taste. We could hear the trio still chatting below when we went to bed, so we thought the likelihood of breakfast at an early hour might be wishful thinking.

The next morning we were up about seven and on going downstairs, found our suspicions confirmed; there was no sign of anyone. In fact it looked like the *Marie Celeste*, everything was just as we had left it, with the exception only of the trio. We returned to our room and made coffee, boiled eggs and sat out on the balcony eating our breakfast, whilst watching the sun come up over the mountains.

As there was still no sign of life downstairs, we went for a walk around the deserted village. We were soon accompanied by a scruffy, medium-sized dog. He appeared to want to take us on a guided tour, because if we did not proceed in his chosen direction, he would nip at our heels until we did. We assumed this was a regular undertaking on his part, as he delivered us back to the guesthouse about thirty minutes later and sat outside looking very pleased with himself.

The trio had now appeared, looking bleary eyed, and were cleaning up and preparing breakfast. Being the polite English couple that we are, we ate another breakfast and then paid our bill and headed off for the gorge.

The Vikos Gorge is quite spectacular, with soaring cliffs either side reaching to some three thousand feet and in some sections it is only fifteen to twenty metres wide. The whole area is beautiful in a very rugged way with forests of oak, beech and pine, rushing mountain streams, with the occasional small village tucked into the folds of the mountains.

That morning, on leaving Papingo, we had crossed an old bridge over quite a broad (but shallow) river, lower down in the valley. Quite near it we had seen a house with a sign outside which just said 'House'! We thought it might be a guesthouse, so we were going to try our luck there for the night. If not, it was only a few miles back to Papingo. Later that afternoon, on arriving there we found a lady standing outside and on speaking to her and finding that she spoke reasonable English, I asked if it was a guesthouse. She looked a little bewildered but said that it was and pointed to the sign as confirmation. She said that she could accommodate us and as she obviously thought that the single word 'house' would enlighten any traveller but the simple-minded, I pursued it no further.

'Pig stew' was on offer for dinner so we asked if we could have some potatoes with it rather than chips. A couple of hours later, when we came down for the meal, the pig stew was very good but the boiled potatoes were stone cold. She had obviously cooked them as soon as we had asked for them. We had a bottle of our own wine as all that was available was a half-bottle of sweet white. Her husband was probably twenty-five years older than his wife and spoke no English. Outside, the road was in the process of being repaired and there was a huge pile of some sort of ballast. We sat for a couple of hours after dinner, watching him fill and remove barrow load after barrow load of this, taking it round to the rear of the house where he was constructing a patio.

It was now nearing the time when we had to meet up with Marylyn and Martin in Thasos, so we made our way back down from the Vikos area to the main northern road. It was approximately four hundred kilometres from joining the road to Keremiti where we would get the ferry to the island. It was, and possibly still is, a fairly lonely road with no large towns until one reached Thessalonika, although there appeared to be a lot of police patrols. Stopping for lunch at a roadside tavern, we entered into a conversation with a Bulgarian professor and his wife who were just on their way home from a holiday in Italy. He said that the police activity was quite usual as there were always Albanian refugees trying to make their way into Greece.

At some stage we joined a short stretch of motorway, which I believe is now complete and links Igoumenitsa with Thessalonika, but to exit where we needed to, meant that we had to go off in what would have been the fast lane, had there been any other traffic at all. Somewhere east of Thessalonika, as dusk was falling, we found a small hotel in a village. I went in to enquire about a room and finding that there was one available, asked about the price. The lady that had met me spoke no English, so not having a pen to hand, drew the price on the wall with her finger. I read it as fifty-two euros, which seemed very expensive for the standard of the place and when I asked to see the room and saw that there was only a cold tap above the sink, it appeared ridiculous. However, as there was a shared bathroom with hot water and as I did not want to press on in the dark, we took it.

Immediately opposite was a small tavern where we had a very good dinner of grilled pork chops, roast chicken, salad and two jugs of wine, for the princely sum of twenty-five euros. At an adjacent table, there was a party of about ten smartly dressed Greeks, celebrating (we imagined perhaps) some sort of anniversary for an elderly couple in the company.

There was also a youngish couple who we had seen coming out of the room next to ours in the hotel. On our return, we heard them come in about an hour later. He then spent the whole night being sick, the soundtrack of which we had no problem in hearing through the paper-thin walls. The following morning, feeling even more aggrieved because of our disturbed night, I went to pay the bill but she only took twenty-five euros from me. She then ushered us back to the tavern where we were fed a nice breakfast of coffee and fried eggs on toast. I have to assume that in marking out the price the night before, she had placed the numerals the wrong way round — life now seemed better!

Thassos

Off we went, reaching Keremiti in time to catch the one fifteen p.m. ferry to Thassos, where we found Marylyn and Martin waiting for us. We liked Thassos – we must have done as we stayed there for three weeks. One of the great pleasures of having time to travel through Europe by car is being able to stop somewhere as long as one wishes and then move on when you are ready.

We had lunch with Marylyn and Martin in a restaurant that they had adopted. It was run by a very pleasant Greek (Vangellis) who was a surprisingly good cook and his girlfriend who couldn't cook at all. Thankfully, she was only ever let loose on breakfasts but as the first one that we tried was disgusting, we didn't bother thereafter.

Marylyn and Martin had found a studio apartment for us. It overlooked the beach and had the usual shower, toilet and cooking facilities and at fifteen euros per night, was more than adequate. Although it is not a place we would bother returning to, on the whole we spent an enjoyable three weeks on the island, which was unusual as we normally try to avoid tourist areas.

A few years after this, we arranged a holiday in Paxos with Marylyn and Martin, flying to Corfu and then by boat. It is a very small island and it was packed. The restaurants were of a poor standard but very expensive, so after two days we had had enough and left for the mainland where we hired a car in Igoumenitsa and spent the rest of our holiday travelling around. Marylyn and Martin spent four or five days with us on the mainland and eventually returned to Paxos in some sort of 'pirate boat', from Parga. In Parga we stayed in the hotel owned by our friend Photas who remembered us from ten or eleven years previously. He said that since that time he had been called on, on two occasions, to help 'lost souls', but both times without police assistance.

A big drawback to Thassos while we were there, was that everywhere seemed to be plagued by wasps, although we were told this was unusual. The island itself is quite small so driving round takes no time at all. Every two or three miles there is another little bay with a couple of tavernas, each full of mainly English holidaymakers, who always stared disbelievingly at a British registered vehicle heading towards them. Vangellis too was fascinated by the Landcruiser and insisted it had all sorts of refinement, such as GPS, that I knew it didn't possess. He appeared to be very disappointed when being allowed to search all over the vehicle for the 'absent extras', he found none. He said, with that look of childish contempt that the Greeks are so adept at, that he intended buying a Landcruiser himself, but he would make sure that it had every extra that it should have.

We continued using his restaurant regularly as the food was good, although we found a couple of others too, until one night after Marylyn and Martin had left, I asked if there was such a thing as a good Greek wine to have with our dinner. He went off saying he had just the thing and returned with a bottle of something called 'Nico Lazaridi' (a blend of Cabernet Sauvignon and Merlot). It was very good, probably one of the best Greek wines that I have tasted. However, when we asked for the bill, we had been charged twenty-five euros for it, which was quite obviously, irritatingly excessive for the quality of the wine. Vangellis had a brother who ran a shop further along the beach. Knowing that he sold wine, the following morning we went in and there was 'Nico Lazaridi' at five euros per bottle; in fact, looking on line twelve years later, one can still buy it for eleven to twelve euros.

Having always been in catering, I am of the opinion that if one doesn't ascertain the cost of something in advance, then it is probably one's own fault if one pays over the odds. There is, of course, something to be said for trusting people to be reasonable, but obviously this doesn't always work.

We stayed on Thassos for a further week but we never returned to Vangellis'. Our apartment was adjacent to his restaurant, with our car parked between the two and in full view. I am sure he would have seen us leaving each evening to dine elsewhere and no doubt would have realised why.

I know Greeks (and Cypriots) fairly well, both from travels in their respective countries and by playing cards and mixing with them in Eastbourne. I like them, they are a friendly and gregarious race and not afraid of hard work. In Eastbourne it was very rare to find a Cypriot as an employee for any length of time, before he had his own business and I never knew one to be unemployed. At the same time, they can be very envious or even disparaging of one another, dependant on the other's perceived success, or lack of it. I suppose it is an immigrant thing. They measure their standing against fellow Cypriots and not necessarily the indigenous population. Having said that, their aim is always to integrate, particularly encouraging their children to do so. One particularly successful Cypriot businessman in Eastbourne, married to an English girl, always believed that our son, Rupert, would be the ideal match for one of his daughters. It never came off but he once told us how offended he was when a fellow Cypriot had suggested his son as a match. His reply, so he told us, was that he didn't agree with interracial marriages and that his daughter would only marry an English boy, and she did.

Back to the Greek Mainland

Leaving Thassos and managing to grab the only *Sunday Times* delivered to the island we decided that prior to heading south we would drive across to Alexandroupoli, the last largish town before the Turkish border. In less than a couple of hours, having driven past 'Alex', we reached the border with Turkey. Without knowing it we had driven through the Greek checkpoint – as there was no one there – and only realised when we saw the Turkish flag and border guards, on reaching their checkpoint. There appeared to be no other traffic at all. We were flagged down and asked for our passports, but producing them I explained that we did not wish to continue into Turkey. I don't think the guard really understood because he looked quite bemused when, having returned our passports, we turned round and headed back to Greece.

Alexandroupoli was very interesting, particularly the lighthouse, which was the main reason for our visit. The lighthouse is positioned in the centre of the seafront and coming from Eastbourne and being used to Beachy Head, it seemed strange to stand underneath while the light flashed above you. We found a hotel (Erika) on the seafront, overlooking both the harbour and railway station. There were dozens of outdoor cafes and tavernas to choose from, none with anything other than menus in Greek and we found no one that spoke any English at all. Choosing one at random, on the basis it was very busy, we had a magnificent meal. They were very helpful and although rushed off their feet, insisted that we went to the kitchen so that we could point out what we wanted. We ended up with 'two shoals' of grilled sardines, followed by stuffed aubergines and beans and then goulash and lamb, both served with a pile of delicious roast potatoes. This being accompanied with a Greek salad and a bottle and a half of wine came to twenty-three euros.

Reluctantly leaving 'Alex' but now only having about nine days before we were due to meet up with our friends in Cyprus, we headed west. Our intention being to reach Mount Olympus area that night, we hugged the coastline as far as Thessalonika, but prior to reaching there, dropped south to drive round Sithonia, the central finger of the three fingers of land that jut out into the Aegean.

Having got lost in Thessalonika (no road signs in English) we navigated our way out by compass and eventually arrived in Agios. Dimitrias, a village near Olympus, at about six pm. Here we found a small hotel at forty euros for bed and breakfast and had a very good dinner of bean soup, wild boar chops and aubergines with potatoes. The next day, having reserved the room for a couple of nights, we set off early to do a reccie of Mount Olympus, with the intention of climbing it the next day. It is possible to drive for about nine kilometres up Olympus and at this point the track to the top starts. Before that, about six kilometres up the road, there is a refuge called Stavros that serves good food.

That evening we had another very good dinner of wild boar steak along with several accompaniments. The following morning, we set off for Olympus, stopping at refuge Stavros for something to take with us for lunch. We had been told (or had read) that from the highest driveable point, where we had been the day before, it was a six-hour walk to the summit, which of course meant a four or five-hour descent. We obviously weren't going to manage this in daylight. However, about three hours up there was a refuge, which meant the descent would take about two hours, so we elected to do this. We did the walk up in the company of a young Canadian (Kyle), who had asked if he could join us. He was an interesting, well-travelled young man but at half our age and a non-stop conversationalist; Gill, who was doing as much talking, found it increasingly difficult to keep up. Eventually we had to suggest that he continued alone.

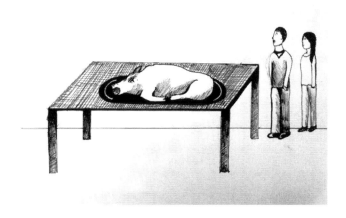

Back to the hotel for dinner, we felt very hungry after our strenuous walk. Tonight's meal was wild boar sausages – we began to see a pattern.

There had been no other guests in the hotel since we had been there but tonight an elderly Greek couple from Athens, who spoke good English, were dining too. No one else in the hotel spoke any English. They explained to us that the owners of the hotel also owned a wild boar farm and that this was the only meat served. Asking what we had eaten the previous two nights, they told us that tomorrow's dinner would be wild boar burger and the following night would be the start of the menu cycle again, which would be wild boar chops!

They told us that they visited ever year for a fortnight and appeared to be quite happy with the repetitive menu. They asked if we would like to see the boar farm and on our agreeing, arranged it with the owners for us. The following morning we were taken by the owners to their farm, which was high up on the side of a mountain and surrounded by fencing. We could see the necessity for this, on being taken into a sort of protected viewing area. There were about sixty to seventy boars all racing down the mountain towards us, biting and jumping at each other. Most seemed to have at least one ear missing and on the whole they appeared pretty vicious.

We stayed one more night at the hotel to complete the food cycle, with the burger and then the next day headed south. We drove down through Elassona and took a small road westward through Deskati to Meteora. Somewhere along the road we spotted a magnificent packhorse bridge over on our left. We stopped to look at it and assumed that it must have been an old route from Elassona to Meteora.

We thought that we might stop in Kalabaka overnight as we had been there before and knew of a nice little hotel with a wonderful view of the famous monasteries, sitting precariously on top of their outcrops of rock. However, as it was only lunchtime, and October 5th (our wedding anniversary) and we needed to be in Cyprus by the 9th, we decided to press on. We drove on for a few hours over a couple of mountain ranges, stopping once to try a hotel. We received no response from knocking at the closed door but as we were about to drive off, a dishevelled fat character in a dirty vest leant out of an upstairs window and shouted something in Greek. Judging from the look of him that his hotel wouldn't be terribly salubrious, we carried on. Somewhere, I think south of Larisa, we went through a ravine where someone was selling fruit on the side of the road. It was starting to get dark and as we had seen no villages for some time, began to think that it might mean another night in the car. However, suddenly, over on our left, perhaps half a mile off the road, we saw what we took to be the lights of a village. We turned off and on eventually reaching it, immediately spotted a tavern with chickens and pork roasting on spits. Going in and speaking to a man behind the counter, and gathering that he had no English, I made the usual signs of sleeping. Understanding what I wanted, he came outside and pointed to a building some two hundred yards away. Off we went and finding it was a little hotel, we booked in.

Within half an hour we were back in the tavern, ready for our anniversary dinner. Unfortunately, we had to wait about an hour for the chicken and pork to be ready but we were happy to savour the aroma, whilst apparently consuming two jugs of wine before the food arrived! When the food did arrive, it was delicious, the owner kept bringing it and we kept eating it, along with another couple of jugs of wine. It was Saturday night so the tavern, only seating about thirty, was full. Being thoroughly sated and no doubt 'flying' a little, Gill and I were toasting each other and giving what we thought was a quiet rendition of *The Flintstones Happy Anniversary*. It could not have been that quiet, as we suddenly realised that the other diners were listening to us. We tailed off in some embarrassment but got a round of applause anyway; and yet another jug of wine, compliments of the owner.

The hotel, which only had about six rooms and, as usual, no other guests, was slightly bizarre in that the bedroom and bathroom were expensively furnished but very badly done. Everything in the bathroom was marble but nothing fitted. The door only opened about twelve inches and then wedged solid on the marble floor. The big marble shower tray could only be accessed by clambering over the loo and had no sort of partition, or even a curtain around it. In the morning, after my having had a shower, the door handle came away in my hand. Gill was listening to Beethoven's Ninth Symphony on the TV and thought that my banging on the bathroom door was part of the percussion, but eventually rescued me.

Leaving for Athens the following morning, I failed to make a note (either in my journal, or on the map) of the location of this village. So although we have been back on two occasions since, and tried to find it, we have not been able to do so. It has become a little like Brigadoon.

Arriving in Athens and making our way to Piraeus, we were disappointed to find that the ferries to Cyprus had stopped operating. We were left with no alternative but to fly to Larnaca, leaving the car at Athens airport. There not being a flight until the following day, we booked into a Sofitel hotel, somewhat more expensive that our normal accommodation (two hundred and sixty-five euros) but only yards from the departure lounge. Because we had dined 'in public', hotels, restaurants, tavernas, for several weeks now, we decided that it would be a change to have dinner in private, in our suite. We ordered from a fairly extensive room service menu and lo and behold, on the wine list was Chateau Nico Lazaridi at eighteen euros a bottle, seven euros less in this four-star hotel than we had paid for it in the tavern in Thassos! Dinner, when it arrived, was wheeled in on a table on which, when the two drop down flaps were raised, everything was set out as in a restaurant.

Cyprus

Landing in Larnaca the following day, we took a taxi to Paphos and as we were now three days in advance of when we were due to meet our friends, took a room in an hotel in the old town for a couple of nights. We spent the next two days visiting people that we knew, both Cypriots and ex-pats while waiting for 'the gang' to arrive. One day, six of us spent a very enjoyable day sailing along the coast, Barbara and John not joining us as Barbara is no seafarer. Lunch (which was included) was to be taken at Lara Bay but as it was fairly rough a number of people left the boat when we called at Coral Bay. At Lara Bay the weather improved so with the exception of Pam, who mooched about looking for more wine, we all went for a swim. Unfortunately, Jim, forgetting to remove his wad of notes from the pocket of his shorts, had to spend the next couple of hours trying to dry out his cash.

On another occasion, Fran and Dave, the fourth couple, hired a car and not having been to Cyprus previously, asked if Gill and I would spend the day with them, showing them some of the country. We set off towards Troodos, taking the mountain road up through Fasoula and at Kithasi, stopped to show them where we had frequently had barbecues by the river. Reaching Platres, we took them into The Forest Park Hotel for coffee. We knew the two brothers who owned this hotel, they also owned an hotel in Nicosia, which I believe was taken over by the UN. The road up from Paphos to Troodos always intrigued me, insomuch as in the winter months one could drive from the equivalent of an English summer's day on the coast, up through orange and cherry blossom groves, to deep snow in the mountains, and all within a couple of hours.

Leaving Forest Park, we drove on through Cedar Valley, this road being a bit repetitive, with its snake-like twists and turns, to Pano Panagia. We had never driven through Pano Panagia previously without being stopped by a very pretty Cypriot lady (married to a Polis policeman) who tried, always unsuccessfully, to sell us lace tablecloths. We saw no sign of her this time but spotted a tavern where we decided to stop for a late lunch. On asking for the menu, the lady owner said that there was no menu on a Sunday but invited us into the kitchen to see what was available. She pointed out some bean soup and what was only a couple of portions of lamb, tomatoes and onions, cooked in the oven. I said that there was only really two portions, to which she agreed but said there was nothing else available. There was no one else in the restaurant as it was about four p.m., although she may have been busy earlier. In any event, we agreed to make do with what she had, along with a Greek salad and a couple of bottles of wine. The meal in itself was enjoyable enough, although we could have eaten more had there been anything more on offer. Towards the end of the meal she plonked down some mouldy grapes and four cakes, which none of us wanted, so these went uneaten.

Asking for the bill, I was presented with a scrap of paper which had a few figures listed and came to a grand total of fifty-five Cyprus pounds. The equivalent of about sixty-eight pounds sterling, an outrageous amount in those days. Querying the figure with her and knowing that the wine was five CYP per bottle, I found that she had charged five CYP for the unwanted and uneaten grapes and cakes and had charged for four main courses instead of the two that we had agreed. To make things worse, she had charged five CYP per portion (twenty-five pounds sterling) for the bean soup, the same price as for the main courses should we have had four.

I refused to pay this extraordinary figure and offered her forty CYP, which was still far too much but she refused this and said she would call the police. After about ten minutes, two policemen turned up and I explained the problem to them. I said that we had been charged for four main courses when she had initially agreed that there were only two and asked them if they had ever heard of bean soup costing five CYP when the average price was one and a half CYP. I also pointed out that we had been given a handwritten bill on a scrap of paper (illegal in Cyprus) which had now mysteriously disappeared and had been replaced with a proper cash receipt. Although one of the policemen was sympathetic and they both quite obviously knew that we had been outrageously overcharged, they said they could do nothing about it and we would have to pay. I refused, so they made a telephone call and passing the phone to me said that it was a senior officer. When I spoke to him, he introduced himself as Inspector 'something or other' and said that if we didn't pay, he would order not only my arrest but all four of us. I had to accept defeat, or at least then, as it seemed unreasonable to have our two friends arrested on their first visit to Cyprus.

The Following Day

I find it difficult to let sleeping dogs lie when I perceive injustice, a flaw in my character, no doubt!

About ten a.m. the following morning, Gill and I (Gill armed with notebook and pencil) went into the tourist office to make a complaint. I explained to the girl behind the counter the problem we had experienced the previous day. She jotted down a few details, without, one has to say, a great deal of interest, and said that if we would like to take a seat, the manager would come out and see us. Half an hour went past and, as nothing had happened, which is what we expected, I went back to the counter and asked if the manager was likely to appear before lunchtime. The young lady said that he was busy but would see us when he had time.

A little encouragement was needed. I explained that I was a freelance travel writer, travelling through Europe and writing articles but with particular emphasis on Cyprus, both because of its popularity with British tourists and also because of its imminent entry into the EU. Things started to happen, we were sat down and brought coffee and out came the manager. We now had their full attention. I asked questions while Gill took shorthand notes. I asked if, when the article was published, they thought that this would give a true reflection of, and or be detrimental to the tourist trade? They apologised profusely and said that they had experienced problems with this same tavern in the past and we were to be assured that the owner would be admonished. They also went on to say that they believed this sort of thing was most unusual in Cyprus. I agreed and pointed out that we had been visitors to the island for over twenty years, but unfortunately the article had to be factual!

Telephone calls were made and I was asked to speak to various people (including the head of the Cyprus Tourist Board) who also wished to apologise. We left it at that, happy that we had got the reaction we wanted.

A day or so later, the holiday came to an end, the gang catching their flight back to the UK and we returned to Athens to pick up the car. Cyprus had changed, quite apart from being ripped off, absolutely unknown in Cyprus prior to then, it had become too commercialised, with hustlers outside some bars and restaurants, trying to entice you in.

We have not been back since.

Kefalonia (and the Spot Sanction)

Continuing our journey from the airport, we set off for Patras to catch the ferry back to Ancona. However, on arriving in Patras and enquiring at the Anek booking office, we were told that the first available first class cabin was two days hence. We decided to spend a few days in Kefalonia and then catching the ferry from Fiscardo to Levkos, drive up that island and across the causeway to the mainland. Continuing on through the new tunnel at Prevesa, up to Igoumenitsa and boarding the ferry to Ancona from there.

We had been to Kefalonia before, spending over a month on the island on one of our previous trips. On this occasion, we drove down to Kilini and took the ferry to Poros. One arriving there we booked into the Oceana Hotel which is high up on the headland, overlooking the harbour. This is a family run hotel, although most of the running appeared to be done by a young lady named Maria, who we believe was the daughter-in-law of the family. Whenever one was in the environs of the hotel, whether on the balcony of our room or down by the pool, a dozen times a day we would hear the cry (screech) 'MARIA' from one member of the family or another. Nevertheless, for us on our last visit it had proved to be a good find, and for dinner there was a small restaurant tucked into the cliff just below, or several tavernas strung along the beach.

We wanted to spend the three days or so visiting our old haunts, Argostoli, Assos, Sami etcetera. On that previous visit we had caught a ferry from Zachynthos (an island we didn't like at all) to Argostoli, booking into a hotel there for a couple of nights. Having had a look round that part of the island, we were not impressed and thought we had made another mistake, as we had by going to Zachynthos. However, on doing a virtual sweep of the island on the second day, we found Poros, Sami, Fiskardo and Assos. Kefalonia, being a fairly large island, did not appear to be too commercialised, with the possible exception of Skala, and although very attractive, Fiskardo.

We decided to move to Assos first and found a small apartment high up overlooking the bay. This was a lovely setting but lacking air conditioning was indescribably hot in the afternoons. On unpacking, Gill discovered a shortage of knickers. Apparently she had washed five or six pairs and hanging them on a curtain rail in the bedroom in Argostoli, had forgotten them! We dropped into a very healthy lifestyle of long, strenuous walks before it became too hot, up to the Venetian (or Roman) fort on a promontory, or in the opposite direction up a winding path which eventually joined the road to Fiskardo. This path had incredibly well-built stone walling (each stone being faced) for a long section of its length. We assumed it to be Roman as it was so perfect and the path itself appeared to provide a direct route from the fort down to the bay and then up to Fiskardo.

Prior to the walk, breakfast was always taken on the balcony as soon as the 'bread man' arrived. This was announced by some sort of klaxon as his van approached down the hill. After the walk, we would spend some time swimming in the bay.

There were two or three taverns in Assos, the best, in our opinion, being Nefelia. The other, which we didn't think as good, was owned by a gregarious character who enjoyed talking about himself a great deal. We would have dinner in Nefelia but did occasionally dine in the other as we had to walk right past and he (the verbose one) was always standing outside and would look most dejected if we didn't go in.

The star attraction at Nefelia's was a rather pretty mongrel dog called Irma. She had a slight limp but always wore a rather fetching red chiffon scarf. She was very friendly and when she saw us heading off for one of our walks, would run out and join us, accompanying us for miles

Irma had an enemy, a canine bully by the name of Spot. Spot (a larger mongrel) resided in a café which was situated at the far end of the breakwater. He obviously felt that this was his domain. If we went down for a coffee on our own, he would keep quiet but if Irma joined us he would start barking and snapping. The final straw was one morning when we had walked round to his café with Irma, but having had the temerity to spend nothing, started to walk back, when he suddenly appeared, yapping and generally being a nuisance. I shooed him off but he snapped at me, that was it, I was determined to fix him.

We drove over to Sami and in a gift shop managed to find a giant water pistol, rather like a sten gun with a strap. That afternoon the three of us went looking for Spot. We sat on a bench at the other end of the jetty from his café, knowing that sooner or later he would be taking his postprandial stroll. Sure enough, we soon saw him trotting along the quay but seeing us he slowed down and approached more warily. I let him get to within ten feet and then fired – too high – the water landed on his back. He looked astonished (Irma looked thrilled) but he quickly turned tail and ran back home. We continued to sit there to see whether he would venture back, this being his only exit route. Sometime later, we saw his master get into his truck at the end of the jetty and start driving towards us. We had seen Spot hanging around, eyeing us from afar and thought he may come past having jumped into the open back of the truck. If so, I might be able to get him as they went past. As the truck approached there was no sign of Spot in the back, but as it passed us we saw his legs trotting along on the far side. He had escaped by guile.

How to get him? It was becoming an obsession but I knew that it had to be done by stealth as he had proved himself a wily adversary.

The following morning, from our balcony and looking through binoculars, I could see Spot in his usual prone position on the side of the quay, between the tables outside his café. I had determined my new plan of attack over dinner (and probably with too much wine) the night before. We walked down to the beach and were soon joined by Irma. I took off my shorts and T-shirt, leaving on just my swimming trunks and slinging the loaded sten gun over my shoulder, waded in. It was probably three or four hundred metres across the harbour so I continued a steady breast stroke so that I could keep an eye on Spot. Some fifty yards from the jetty, I saw his head come up from his slumbers, probably attracted by a number of his customers talking and pointing at me. He had obviously recognised me because, as I got closer, he stood up but continued staring intently in my direction. As I reached the quay, and clambered out, he started backing away and when I pulled the sten gun round to fire, he took off at a tremendous speed. Much to my disappointment, the 'jet' didn't quite reach him. "Well, that seemed like a wasted effort," said someone sitting at one of the tables.

"It wouldn't have been if you hadn't woken him up," I replied.

"Are you going to swim back now?" another asked.

"No," I said, "I've provided enough amusement for one morning." With that and still out of breath, I strode off as nonchalantly as possible round the quay with my gun slung over my shoulder.

Later that afternoon, having just finished lunch in Irma's tavern, we saw Spot go trotting past for his postprandial tour. He saw us but knew that he was quite safe if he kept his distance. As soon as he was out of sight, Gill, myself and Irma ran down the quay to Spot's café. We walked in between the tables and Irma and I continued round the corner of the building to the very end of the jetty where we were out of sight. The new plan was that whilst Irma and I stayed hidden from view, Gill, who was now in disguise (wide brimmed hat and sunglasses) and having ordered a coffee, sat at a table where she had a view of the full length of the jetty. We in turn could see Gill from our position and didn't have long to wait. "He's just on his way back," said Gill. She continued, "Fifty yards away, twenty, ten, he has just lain down in his usual place between the tables." I cautiously peered round the edge of the building and saw Spot in his usual somnolent position. Having obviously not recognised Gill and oblivious to my presence, he was therefore unaware of his pending doom.

I pushed Irma slightly forward so that just her head was protruding round the corner and at this point, Gill clicked her fingers to attract Spot's attention. "He's spotted Irma," said Gill, so I pulled Irma back. "He's up and coming round," said Gill out of the corner of her mouth. He suddenly appeared, not two feet away. I fired and got him right between the eyes. His ears flapped like an elephant's and the look of astonishment reappeared on his face, quickly followed by indignation and then fear. He obviously couldn't retrieve his wits because he continued to stand there for a few seconds looking bewildered, time enough to give him another blast! This time he yelped and turned tail, taking off at speed but not fast enough to avoid another jet right up his backside. In his haste, he raced through the tables and chairs, knocking over a couple, which brought his master out to see what was amiss. Not having seen what had transpired, he just looked with some bemusement at his dog haring off down the jetty! He gave us a suspicious look but Gill just smiled sweetly at him and off we went. Honour was satisfied, revenge is sweet and worth biding one's time over! We saw little of Spot after that.

We really enjoyed our stay in Assos, but as it became hotter (June into July) we decided to move on in search of some air conditioning.

We found this at the aforementioned Oceanea Hotel in Poros. We were shown to a lovely room which overlooked the harbour and so were able to see the ferries from Kilini arriving and departing. As previously mentioned, we were very pleased with this small hotel. I think the B and B tariff was about thirty-five euros, with a good choice of breakfast. The little tavern tucked into the cliff underneath the hotel was run by two girls and the 'granny'. The food was good and varied and the granny would, when asked, always collect some sort of green vegetable for us, which grew wild on the cliff. One of the girls would play guitar and sing once everyone had been served.

The hotel seemed remarkably quiet, apart from our immediate neighbours who were Russian and would start drinking coffee and vodka on their balcony about 7 am. The other guests were a Greek family (parents and two young boys). The younger (about ten) would greet us each morning with the salutation, 'Smell my feet'. His mother, who spoke reasonable English, explaining that the older boy had taught him this. She in turn, tried to correct him by telling him it should be 'My feet smell'! The day they left the hotel (by ferry) we happened to be sitting on our balcony watching its departure, when we suddenly heard a cry "Smell my feet," shouted from a hundred feet or so below. There was also a lone English lady from Brighton, but who now lived in Rome. She claimed to be the sister of a well-known model of the 1960s and a direct descendant of Boudicca!

Apart from the family and the English lady, no one else appeared to use the quite large swimming pool, so we were able to take full advantage of it.

Poros was a very enjoyable base and the air conditioning a godsend. I also managed to find a shop where the owner obligingly ordered me a *Sunday Times* for the four Sundays that we were there. I knew that he would not forget to order it as each time we passed his shop, he would shout from the interior, "Good morning Mr Sunday Times."

Returning then to our few days spent in Kefalonia in 2002, we revisited a few of the places, Assos, Argostoli etcetera. Maria claimed to remember us and Irma seemed very pleased to see us and even accompanied us on a short walk. Spot, we saw eyeing us from a distance. I suspect our return had confirmed his worst fears!

At the end of our short stay, we took our planned route to Igoumenitsa to join the ferry.

Our last night in Greece prior to our departure for Italy, was spent at the Aktion Hotel. George greeted us like old friends but on my showing him the sink plug that we had purchased since our last visit some weeks previously and jokingly asked if there was a discount for bringing our own, a look of incomprehension crossed his face. In fact, it was not dissimilar to the expression on Spot's face when I got him between the eyes! I pursued it no further. However, on our return from dinner at the tavern round the corner, we were greeted by George who proudly showed us an array of spare sink plugs on his reception desk, with the comment, "See, no problem, no discount!"

Italy

On our first night back in Italy we stayed in Riccione at, I think, The Sarti Hotel. This was a lovely place, managed again by two brothers. Excellent food, a dinner of tagliatelle bolognese, followed by a veal cutlet. For breakfast one of the two brothers insisted on cooking bacon and eggs for us. The total bill for the night, including gins, wine and brandy was one hundred and forty euros.

Leaving Riccione, we drove back up the autostrada to Modena and once again stayed at the Hotel Eden, eating that night in the wonderful Pizzaria Nelson. Our intention was to continue on into Switzerland but having enjoyed the Italian food so much in the past two nights, and having got used to decent coffee again after the coffee deserts of Greece and Cyprus, we decided to stay in Italy a few days longer. Heading south from Modena, we drove into the Emilia-Romagna region, a very mountainous and forested area, with a ski resort at Abetone. The roads are very narrow and winding and at one point a group of about ten cars, with blaring horns, streamers and loud music playing, presumably a wedding party, careered out of a side road and surrounding us, carried us along for several miles at the sort of speed that only Italians would drive at, before turning off! We eventually came into a small town called San Marcello and seeing an hotel which had the appearance of a concrete block (with the occasional window) booked in there.

Ricardo, the owner, who put us in mind of Mr Bean, spoke very good English but, although being about forty, was absolutely ruled by and terrified of his mother. She was, without doubt, a dragon, chastising him frequently and beadily watching us (the only guests) quite obviously convinced that we were going to pinch the silver.

On the map, I had spotted a Mt Cimone as being the highest point at 2,165 metres and not far from it a village called Fellicarollo. We wanted to do some walking again as we had done little since leaving Thassos.

Driving up to Fellicarollo, which I think is at an altitude of about 3,000 feet, we found a small albergo called Rondinara. Once again we had dropped lucky. It was family owned, Ferdinand and Ornella, son

Stefano and Uncle Sekonda. The three men all spoke good English, Ferdinando and Stefan both being pilots with Air Italia. Ornella (the cook) spoke no English at all but much to the amusement of the other guests, all Italian, came out of the kitchen each evening and in voluble Italian, told us what was available on the menu that night. She would then look at us expectantly until we were rescued, usually by Stefano. The food was excellent rural Italian at its best with lots of various fungi dishes, and in fact for a week in September, they hold a fungi festival. We were made extremely welcome, Stefano said the last English people to have found their way up the mountain had been ten years previously. They too, despite our protestations, insisted on cooking us bacon and eggs each morning. These were always served with a flourish by Fernando (in a skillet straight from the top of the oven) with the comment, "English people like bacon and eggs!"

We spent four days at Rondinara, taking several walks in the mountains and trying desperately to shed some of the pounds that were added each day with pasta and bacon and eggs. One of the walks started for a long stretch, possibly a mile or more, up an old and perfectly cobbled Roman road, which appeared to continue straight into the mountains. On one occasion on our way back to the albergo, passing a cottage near the top of the village, we were invited in by an old man. He and his wife spoke no English but sat us down in the kitchen and plied us with homemade limoncello and cake. Not being able to speak any Italian, we were unable to find out why they were so hospitable but Stefan told us later that they had asked him if we were English.

Although we would have liked to have stayed longer (we have been back since) we still had a long way to go and the attraction of Switzerland was becoming too great to resist. Our total bill at Rondinara for four nights, including all meals and drinks came to the equivalent of two hundred pounds sterling.

Switzerland

If any motorway can be said to be splendid or beautiful, the N2 running up from Milano into Switzerland must rank very highly. The view as one sweeps up towards the Alps must be one of the most spectacular scenes in Europe.

We were going to spend a couple of days in Grindalwald, so having gone back through the Gotthard Pass, we took the road over the Sustanpass and down through Meiringen and Interlaken. We had been to Grindalwald on two previous occasions but only staying for one night each time. Both times we had stayed at The Kreus and Poste, a largish hotel facing the Eiger and adjacent to the railway station. This time however, we were going to try a small hotel called Blümlisalp, which was the last hotel but one at the head of the valley, under the Wetterhorn. Surprisingly no one spoke English at the hotel but we managed to get a top floor room (no lift) with a wonderful view of both the Eiger and the Wetterhorn from the balcony.

We had a very good dinner, rosti, the best I have ever eaten and the breakfast buffet being equally good, we decided to stay a few days longer than planned. Over the next two or three days we did a lot of walking, the first day catching the cable car to First, walking up to the lake and then all the way back down to the hotel via Bort. The following day we did the 'Eiger walk' from the Eiger Gleisher Station down to Grund, about four and a half hours with stops for lunch. The Eiger Gleisher Station is situated just before the train enters the tunnel into the Eiger itself. The train journey (on a route constructed in 1912) is not to be missed. Taking the train up from Grindalwald, one changes trains at Kleiner Schiedegg and very soon you enter the tunnel which winds round and up within the Eiger. There are a couple of stops within the mountain itself where there are viewing windows over the Grindalwald valley, from an elevation of about 9,000 feet. One of these areas has access out onto the mountain, which has been used for rescuing climbers in difficulty on the north face. The train continues climbing until the station within Jungfrau (at about 3,500 metres) is reached. Here there is a huge complex of restaurants and shops, viewpoints and access onto the mountain, in good weather. The best place to eat is the most expensive, but not madly so, overlooking the longest glacier in Europe.

There are several 'longests' in Grindalwald. Already mentioned, the longest glacier, the longest cable car run (to Männlichen) and not to be missed, the longest toboggan run, nine or ten kilometres. For this, one of the tyre-chained ski buses is taken up to Bussalp from where one can hire a sledge and toboggan back down the same route to Grindalwald. Halfway down there is a small bar which serves grog and mulled wine. The run can be very fast in places, with sharp bends and in fact the second time we did this run, Gill managed to misjudge a bend but fortunately hit a crash barrier. This was actually Christmas 2003, and apart from a badly bruised knee, it also knocked Gill's confidence to the extent that she couldn't participate again.

The following day we had booked to go to Schilthorn (this mountain has a revolving restaurant on top) which meant a number of changes of trains, cable cars and funiculars. On our return, we should have changed trains at Zweilutschinen but as it was dark didn't realise that we had arrived at the station. Suddenly noticing where we were, I jumped up and shot off the train, forgetting Gill could only hobble. The train pulled out before Gill had a chance to alight and for some reason it didn't occur to me to jump back on. About an hour later she reappeared having had to travel as far as Wilderswil before she could return.

Another not to be missed experience, is a helicopter trip from just down the valley below Grindalwald. This lasts about forty-five minutes to an hour and takes you over the shoulder of the Eiger and across the permanent ice fields behind, returning via Jungfrau.

The Blümlisalp was a wonderful find, we have been back many times since 2002, Christmas and New Year, summer and spring. We paid one hundred and forty Swiss francs (SF) for bed and breakfast that first time, I think about eighty five pounds sterling, depending on the exchange rate. It has been quite a bit less than that sometimes but usually not much more. Switzerland appears to have no inflation. The most recent occasion that we have stayed at Blümlisalp was over Christmas and New Year 2012/13. We paid one hundred and sixty five Swiss francs for the same room; the total bill for ten nights including all dinners and drinks being just under three thousand Swiss francs, approximately two thousand pounds sterling. As a comparison, in our last year at Devonshire Park Hotel (2001) we were charging one thousand pounds per couple (excluding drinks) for four nights over the Christmas period.

The owner of Blümlisalp (Andreas Lohner) is one of the most contented human beings I have ever met. He is the head chef, smokes a large Swiss pipe (outside the kitchen) and appears to have a new girlfriend each time we visit. In the winter he clears snow with his own small snowplough, whilst puffing on his pipe and is followed everywhere by his Alsatian dog. He took me into the kitchen on one occasion to show me how to make rösti correctly and makes a point after each dinner to come out and ask us, "Is good?" The extent of his spoken English.

It was now approaching the end of October, so we decided to start heading south. In February of 2002 we had bought a penthouse apartment (off plan) in Mijas, Spain, so we were going down to see how it was progressing. Why we bought a property in Spain rather than Switzerland will be an eternal mystery to us. We like Spain very much, although not necessarily as much as Switzerland. What we particularly enjoy about Spain is travelling through it, staying in small hotels (hostals) and not being stuck in one place. Staying in one place in Switzerland is different, there is always lots to do, winter or summer, so long as one enjoys the great outdoors. The cost of property was not really a factor either. Certainly at that time, one could have bought a similar sized property in Switzerland for about the same price.

France

Taking the route over the Susten Pass, we headed down through Sion and Chamonix towards Grenoble. We intended driving into Zermatt to see the Matterhorn but as it was pouring with rain and very misty, gave it a miss. From Grenoble we dropped down into Gap and stayed at an Ibis overnight. Continuing the next day, we arrived in Avignon and booked into an hotel in the centre for two nights.

We were not impressed with Avignon. Obviously the bridge was impressive and so were the town walls but dinner, both nights, were touristy and rubbishy; with the French being rather more rude than usual, if that's possible.

What is it about the French? They have wonderful countryside, mountains, forests and rivers – skiing and some of the best beaches in Europe. They have the best of wines and food (with some exceptions), beautiful women and Jacques Tati, and yet they are rude and miserable. Not all of course, but a far greater percentage than any other European nation.

They are perverse in the sense of being contrary and obstinate, but particularly in the sense that if you speak some French (but aren't fluent) you are likely to receive shorter shrift than if you speak none at all!

Leaving Avignon and linking up with the A9, we arrived at a roadside service area called Catalan Village, which is on the border with Spain. We had lunch and got chatting to the manager who spoke very good English, was amenable (unlike most of his countrymen) and had an old dog called Wellington. Because of the combination of these virtues and as it was a lovely place, we stayed for the night. In our conversation with Wellington's master, Andorra had cropped up and he asked us if we had ever been there, saying it was well worth a visit if we hadn't.

Andorra

Deciding therefore to detour through Andorra, we backtracked up to Perpignon and then took a very winding mountain road (N116) up into Andorra. Entering a village called Soldeu, we saw over on our right a small hotel immediately opposite what looked like a ski slope. We booked into the hotel for two nights on demi pension basis at the extremely reasonable price of seventy euros for two, the equivalent of about fifty pounds. Enquiring about the ski slope, we were told that's what it was (in the winter) and that there was a ski station with a restaurant at the top.

Next day we set off up the slope, intending to have lunch and then walk back down a road that meandered from the valley up to the ski station. Walking up a ski slope is very hard going, there is no deviating from side to side as one normally does on a mountain, it is just continuously straight up! However, after about three hours we eventually reached the top and sure enough, there in the distance, we could see the station and a restaurant with people inside. Entering the restaurant we saw that it was self-service, so picking up a couple of trays, joined the queue. As we neared the counter we could see some very appetising dishes for a coldish October day. Paella, roast chicken and pork chops in sauce and quite a lot besides. Reaching the front of the queue, I ordered two bean soups and two main courses from the lady serving. She said something in Spanish, so assuming she had not understood me, I pointed to the dishes that we wanted. However, seeing a look of consternation crossing her face, I realised something was amiss. Along came another lady who, speaking a little English, explained to us that the restaurant was not open to the public until the ski season started, a couple of months hence, and that they were only serving staff from the ski station. Probably looking crestfallen, we apologised and started to move away from the counter but were called back and told that we could eat if we wished. We ordered our food and in the meantime, someone cleared a table for us, placing on it a jug of water and a bottle of wine. The food was excellent and with a pudding included, the total bill came to eleven euros.

Andorra then must have been the least expensive place in Europe. Heading into Spain the day that we left, we managed to buy some Tanqueray gin at eight pounds per bottle and Beefeater gin at five pounds – unbelievable.

Spain

Driving down through the Pyrenees into Spain, we travelled through some beautiful countryside. Having reached Lleida, we joined the coastal motorway near Tortosa and continued down past Castello, stopping overnight at La Plana. We have stopped at this motorway service area a number of times and very often after dinner, have sat under some five or six enormous palm trees set in a group at the side of the motorway, trying but failing to imagine what it would have been like prior to the motorway having been constructed, when they probably sheltered a shepherd from the midday sun.

Instead of continuing down the coast road (which is pretty boring) we now swung inland through the wine-growing area of Requena. There are some quite nice wines from here but some of the best Spanish wines I have tasted, apart from the obvious Riojas and Navarres, are from a little known area called Priorat, west of Barcelona. They are, on the whole, fairy expensive, some very, but are deep, full-bodied wines, strong at fourteen to fifteen per cent, and compare favourably to any others in their price range, Spanish, French or Italian. After spending a few hours in the Requena area, we continued south on the road to Albacete but driving through a little town called Casas Ibanaz we spotted a small hotel in the main street – Hotel Aros.

Hotel Aros was a very good find and we have been back a few times since. It is run by two brothers (I think) both very pleasant although neither speaks much English. There is a huge bar at the front of the hotel serving locals, with a big variety of tapas at lunch and dinner. At the rear, there is a very pleasant (and at weekends, busy) restaurant where the best Iberico ham I have ever tasted is served, along with myriad dishes of an excellent standard. The last time we stayed there was in 2011, when two night's accommodation with dinner and drinks, cost two hundred euros. On that occasion there was a slightly embarrassing incident in the restaurant. Gill and I have this rather silly game, whereby, when having dinner, if one can distract the other's attention in some way, one then takes a slurp of the other's wine. Childish I know! This time I had managed to distract Gill and having taken my slurp, was suddenly aware of several mutterings of 'Mujar', which I knew to mean wife in Spanish.

Adjacent to us was a table of about eight Spanish ladies, all of whom were glaring at me with what can only be described as feminine (sisterly) indignation. Needless to say, Gill found this very amusing, knowing that not speaking Spanish there was no way I could explain that it was just a daft game that we play.

On that visit, we drank a particularly good local wine recommended by the 'restaurant brother'. It was a Cabernet Sauvignon but unfortunately I have forgotten the name, However, we managed to find some (at six euros a bottle) in a wine co-operative in the main street.

The countryside around Casas Ibanaz is rather flat and uninteresting and in fact the small town itself – which bizarrely has a Chinese emporium – puts me in mind of somewhere in Mexico, where one wouldn't be surprised to see brushwood rolling down the main street! However, the route prior to it, between Teruel, Libros and Requena is very pretty.

One morning, deciding not to bother with breakfast, we went out for a walk about nine a.m., intending to have coffee while we were out (which we did) and to return in time for lunch. Arriving back at midday, we went to the local's bar and finding a table, sat down and waited while they finished bringing out the tapas to the counter. I saw the 'bar brother' pointing us out to a young waitress and five minutes later she appeared with large tray of coffee, toast, jams and pastries. We had to eat it and then wait a decent length of time before ordering tapas and a bottle of wine.

Heading south-west from Casas Ibanez eventually towards Alcaraz, the terrain is again fairly flat but one does get the impression of what a huge country Spain is. Continuing on the main road to Riopar the Sierra de Alcaraz is soon reached and taking a right turn out of the village on a small road (CM3204) one is soon driving along the beautiful valley of the Rio Guadalima. We had a picnic lunch by the side of the river, of freshly baked bread, Iberico ham (bought in Alcaraz) wine and with tomatoes that had a taste no English tomato has ever aspired to, let alone achieved. We were joined for lunch by a herd of some twenty goats who had wandered down the hillside apparently for this express purpose.

Following the road, eventually a large lake is reached at Canada Morales and on the right is Hostal Losan. This area is the Sierra de Segura and with the exception of the Picos de Europa, is as pretty as anywhere in Spain — think Shropshire compared to the Lake District. At Hostal Losan (having ordered it the night before) we ate the best paella ever. Cooked to perfection, it contained pork, rabbit, chicken and chorizo, along with prawns, moules and baby clams. We tried to order a first course but the owner dissuaded us on the basis that we wouldn't do justice to the paella. He was quite right.

There was no one else staying in the hostal but it had the usual public bar in which there were always a few locals. Sitting outside having a pre-dinner drink whilst waiting for our paella, we noticed two ladies talking in the bar. One of them had a pushchair (with a baby in it), which she was gently pushing backwards and forwards. As the conversation became more and more animated, so the pushchair moved to and fro faster and faster. All of a sudden, the baby shot out, somehow going under the retaining strap and hurtled at tremendous velocity across the shiny, tiled floor, only stopping when she or he was fielded by a quick-thinking man at the bar!

The lake, which is about twenty kilometres in length, has two other hotels along its shore and at the southern end is a Parador. We have stayed in a number of Paradors over the years and although they are usually of a very good standard, one does not feel in touch with Spain in them. This of course is true of any big hotel in any country. It obviously depends on what one wants from travel but our preference in Spain is for hostals. Many English people that we have spoken to, especially those living in Spain, appear to think that hostals are something akin to a youth hostel or even a 'down and outs' hostel. We have met people in Mijas who would rather drive the six hundred miles from Bilbao or Santander in one go, rather than venture into one. And yet they are of reasonable standard, about the same as a Travel Lodge, always with an en suite bathroom, spotlessly clean and with bags of character with their polished olive wood interiors. Where they do differ from Travel Lodges or Premier Inns, is in the type of food served. Nearly all of them serve a three course meal, with a good choice, rather than the ubiquitous fried this and fried that. The cost seems to be very much the same everywhere (thirty-five to forty-five euros for a double room) and twenty-five euros (including a bottle of wine) for two, for dinner. They are on a par with Ibis and Campanile in France but a little less expensive. There are also posadas (inns). These are usually small concerns and were originally basic accommodation for travellers, carriers, rural workers et cetera. Many of these are now quite smart but we have stayed in one or two in which the only thing that had changed is the different generations of owners.

Spanish people on the whole are very friendly and at times can be quite endearing. One lunchtime, sitting outside the bar of Hostal Losan, having a beer, I was sorting through a pocketful of loose change that I always seem to accumulate. The only other person sitting on the patio was an old chap who looked like a farmer. I noticed that he had been watching me and he suddenly called for the owner. When the owner appeared, the old man said something in Spanish and the owner came across to us. He said that the old man wanted to buy us a drink as he obviously thought I was checking to see whether or not I could afford another one. We thanked him but politely refused, so he insisted I have a cigarette which, although I don't smoke. I felt obliged to accept!

Leaving the lake, we spent one more night before going on to Mijas in a posada in the village of Capileira, the highest village in the Sierra Nevada.

Arriving at El Limonar about midday, we found that not a great deal of progress had been made on the property and in fact it was to be another fourteen months before we could finally move in. The purchase of this property eventually ended up as a financial disaster, with a loss to us of something in the region of a hundred and fifty thousand euros.

There are friendly, hospitable Spanish people and then there are estate agents, solicitors and developers. One should be wary of all these, although of course they are not all of the same ilk, we may have just been unlucky. The cost of our penthouse was two hundred and sixty five thousand euros, which including fees and taxes ended up at two hundred and ninety-five thousand euros. We furnished it for some thirty-five thousand euros, making a grand total of three hundred and thirty thousand euros. On exchange of contracts, we were asked by our solicitor (who eventually ended up in prison for, I think, money laundering) for about ten per cent in cash. We flatly refused to do this, firstly because although apparently accepted practice, it was illegal and secondly, it would, on our wishing to sell, have created an immediate capital gain which was taxable at about eighteen per cent. To cut a long story short, we finally managed to sell for two hundred and fifty thousand euros (including furnishings) but less fees and taxes, a huge capital loss. Three percent of this figure (seven thousand five hundred euros) had to be paid over to the Spanish government in lieu of a possible capital gain. We should then have been entitled to reclaim this figure when the transaction was completed and that it could be shown that no capital gain had been made. However, not only were we refused when our solicitor tried to reclaim this money but were told that we were liable for a further three per cent (CGT) up to a sale price of, if my memory serves me correctly, three hundred and thirty thousand euros. The reasoning behind this was that it had been sold for less than the current value and also presumably because it was assumed that we had paid cash up front. Neither of these assumptions were correct of course. We had, as already mentioned, refused to pay any part in cash and had marketed the property for three years (originally at three hundred and thirty thousand euros) before selling in 2007 at the best price we could get in an ever-plunging market. To put the fall of property values in perspective, our neighbours in the adjacent penthouse are still trying to sell their property at one hundred and seventy-five thousand euros.

Although we like Fuengirola (and still do) with its plethora of good Spanish restaurants, mostly hidden in the side streets, away from the touristy seafront, the lifestyle was not for us. We met a lot of very nice people (expats) but after a few months decided that the continuous drinking was probably not a good idea. Neither was the area conducive to walking, whatever George Borrow and Laurie Lee made of it. It was too arid for Gill and me. The expats had formed a walking club and seemed to particularly enjoy a walk down a dry river bed, from Mijas to the coast. We found this quite bizarre as to us it appeared to be nothing more than a stroll along a giant ditch!

The drinking mentioned above sometimes became monumental sessions. They could last from midday when a group of us would meet up in a restaurant for lunch and then having had dinner at a different venue, usually end up at someone's apartment until early the following morning. The ringleader of this particular 'merry club' was a retired pathologist, who one would have thought would be the one person who would have been aware of the likely consequences of the excess. Gill and I were not averse to this occasionally but we neither wanted its regularity nor were we, in fact, capable of it!

Of course, not all the people we met indulged to this extent, and in fact there was a good social life to be had. There were lots of dinner parties as everyone was interested in making new friends. At one of our dinner parties, we invited a cross section of known drinkers and one couple who were known to be reasonably moderate. I happened to notice that the husband was unusually drinking quite heavily and by the time we had reached the coffee stage, was heavily hooded eyed. The table mats we had bought had a quite realistic design of a cup and saucer as their motif. On Gill mentioning coffee, but prior to actually serving it, we all watched in fascination as he attempted time and time again to pick up the picture of the cup from the place mat! He was only stopped in this fruitless exercise by Gill placing a cup of coffee in front of him. But unfortunately, now being faced by what he thought were two cups, he knocked the real one over.

Among others, another memorable occasion of our own excesses was a weekend that we spent in Nerja. On our first visit to Spain in 1997, we had stayed there and discovered several restaurants strung along the beach, below the cliffs. One of these in particular, on Sunday lunchtimes, served a choice of paella or roast pork for about four pounds. Having had your first plateful one could return for more as many times as you wished. Whilst staying in Mijas, we decided to spend a weekend in Nerja. Arriving on the Saturday, we found a very nice little hostal where we booked in for two nights. On the Saturday night we had an excellent dinner in a game restaurant in the centre of town, all perfectly civilised. On the Sunday we walked down to our beach restaurant round about midday, to make sure of getting a table. We had first courses of fried prawns, followed by several plates of pork and paella. As it was a beautiful late October or early November day, it seemed a nice idea to extend the lunch as long as possible and so ordered another bottle of wine at each course. I'm not certain of the eventual total of the number of bottles although I do remember two or three. Late afternoon as the sun sank lower, most people had drifted off and the solitary guitar player appeared to be playing just for us. We had an enormous brandy and a coffee to round off 'lunch' and then decided to stretch out on a couple of sunbeds on the beach immediately opposite, to catch the last of the sun. It was probably two or three hours later when we woke, everywhere was deserted and it was dark, although moonlit. As it was only about eight thirty p.m., we decided that rather than go back to the hostal, we would follow the 'Rope Walk' along the beach and climbing the steps up the cliffs, have a coffee and cake at a little bar that we had discovered the previous evening. The Rope Walk was a collection of rope bridges and steps, strung along the base of the cliffs under Nerja, which we had been along a couple of times in 1997. However, on arriving at the beginning of the obstacle course, we found it blocked by a huge piece of concrete some eight to nine feet high, with a sign to the effect that it was closed. Undeterred, Gill clambered up on my shoulders and hauled herself up and over while I managed to climb up the side. Unfortunately though, as we started to progress along what was now a very overgrown path, we could see that a lot of the bridges and steps had collapsed. Undaunted we continued, but it meant clambering down into gullies and up small rock faces and through the type of prickly vegetation that is indigenous to Spain. It took us about an hour and a half rather than the twenty minutes that we remembered. On eventually reaching the bar, we must have looked quite a sight covered in dust and with lacerated legs as we were both wearing shorts. The two boys that ran the bar recognised us from the previous evening but greeted us with some consternation at the difference in our appearance. One of them brought out a bowl of water and a clean cloth so that we could wipe off some of the dust and blood. On our previous visit I had assumed

the boys were gay as one of them was quite camp but, watching the loving way that he wiped over Gill's thighs while she ate cake and drank coffee, I wasn't so sure. I had to clean my own legs!

Leaving El Limonar – Mijas.

Early in December we left Mijas to drive to Santander to catch the ferry home. The first night we only managed as far as Alora, having spent the day exploring the Parque Natural, near Ronda. Arriving in the town about five or six p.m., we were held up in a traffic jam which was being organised (or made more chaotic) by a policeman who waved his arms and constantly blew a whistle, but to no effect. As I was right by him, I asked the whereabouts of a hostal. He stopped all the traffic including an old man on a moped, who had strings of onions wrapped around his shoulders rather like a bandolier. He spoke to the old man who appeared to remonstrate with him a little but then coming back to us said, "Follow," pointing to the onion seller. We duly did as instructed and were eventually taken to a hostal in a lovely position high above the town. The old man rode off before we could thank him.

The following day, we continued northwards towards Cordoba. The lakes at Guadalhorce, just west of Antequira are certainly worth a visit but north of there the terrain flattens out quite substantially, leading to an area of wide open plains. Somewhere here, but unfortunately I can't remember where, we entered a small village in the late afternoon. We decided to stop there if we could find somewhere to do so. This was difficult as there were no hostals, and posadas very often have no signs or something very small. In the village square we came across a parked police car with two policemen seated in it, leisurely smoking. I thought that I may as well try the same ruse as the previous evening, so stopping by them said, "Señors, hostal/posada por favour?" They directed us to follow them and in a short space of time pulled up outside a very small posada. Going in, we were shown upstairs to a room which had another room immediately opposite and a shower and toilet in between the two. In this other room, the door being open, we could see four men sitting on the lower bunks of twin bunk beds, playing cards on a chair in between. It was obvious that we all used the same shower and toilet but later, having heard them showering, I went to check it out for Gill and found it to be spotless, as in fact was our bedroom. The cost for two of us was twelve euros.

We had gathered from the lady owner when we arrived, that we could have dinner but not breakfast. Looking out of our bedroom window, we had spotted a small bar just opposite, so about six p.m. we went across for a pre-dinner drink. Although they are now few and far between, there are still places in Spain where one is served a little tapas with each drink, happily this was one of them. We were given some dark Iberico ham on French bread, two small meatballs and some fried fish, which we think was rosada.

Returning to the posada about seven p.m., we found two tables only, in what was probably her sitting room. The one table was occupied by the four card players from upstairs, all strangely in pyjamas. We had a very good meal of homemade soup followed by a fresh tortilla and salad. Along with a litre of wine, this cost the same as the accommodation – twelve euros. The quartet went to bed long before us and at about four a.m. the following morning, we heard them getting up and leaving. Later in the morning, we drove past some road menders, two of whom Gill recognised as our fellow guests in the posada.

Going downstairs the following morning at about eight a.m., we found no signs of life and everything more or less as we had left it the night before. Leaving our overnight bag, we went back across to the little bar in search of breakfast. We were greeted like old friends and given two huge cups of strong coffee. I made eating gestures to 'le patron' and he fetched two pastries for us. Neither of us, and me in particular, are very keen on sweet things at breakfast so I tried again. I asked for, "Toast, por favor," which he understood and readily did for us but accompanied with two dishes of different types of jam. Pointing to the jam I said, "No gracis Senor," so he took away the one I was pointing at! I again said, "No, Senor," pointing at the remaining jam, so this was taken away but replaced with the first dish. By this time, the three of us along with a couple of locals were all finding our inability to communicate very amusing. I made 'savoury noises' and Gill said 'jamon', and suddenly it all became clear. From under the counter he produced a pot of something that looked like pink dripping. This is what it proved to be, pork dripping with smokcd pimento blended in and with some pimento left in small pieces. He also fetched us some of the delicious Iberico that we had had the night before. The pork dripping was just the thing for a savoury breakfast, we had never come across this before although we have had it many times since. In fact later, when we eventually were able to move into our apartment, we found a small restaurant (the pork and lard restaurant) just outside Mijas that served this dripping as a first course, coated on thin slices of roast pork fillet, mouth-watering! Of course, not everyone would find it delicious, some no doubt would find it disgusting. We once took our son and his partner (Kelly) up to the 'pork and lard' restaurant, she found it revolting exclaiming, "I can't believe your parents eat lard." She was a vegetarian at the time! At a later date, on a visit to see them at their home in Nottingham, much to their amusement, my first course at dinner came out as half a pound of lard on a plate, still in its wrapping.

Heading north after having been back to the posada to pay and collect our bag (the lady owner was still in her dressing gown and hairnet) we eventually reached Cordoba and then spent some time meandering past lakes and into the Sierra Morena at Villanueva. Our intention was to spend one night in this mountain range (a beautiful area) and then head north-east to join the main north/south central motorway – A, E5 (now 1V/E5) – south of Madrid.

In our travels back and forth across Spain, we had stayed two or three times at a hostal (Guzmann) at Dos Barrios on this highway. It was conveniently situated halfway between Santander and Malaga, three hundred miles from each. Although the surrounding area, with the exception of Toledo, is fairly flat and uninteresting, I always find it somewhat difficult when driving across the central plain of Spain, to reconcile the fact that it is over two thousand feet above sea level.

Continuing north from Villanueva, we eventually reached and crossed the Rio Guadiana and soon after this we reached a village (possibly Arroba but I'm not sure) and immediately spotted a small posada. Here it was the opposite of the night before, we could have breakfast but not dinner. However, just opposite was again a small bar in which we were once again fed various tapas with our drinks. Asking the barman about the possibility of a meal, with the aid of my usual eating gestures, along with the word 'comida', I received a shake of the head. However, he then drew a little map on a napkin showing the bar and at about two hundred metres another building, alongside which he wrote the word 'comida'. Off we went in search of dinner.

Finding the building shown, it appeared to be a community hall of some description. On entering, it certainly looked like a community hall but had a wonderful aroma of spit-roasted pork. The place was deserted, with the exception of a man behind the counter basting the pork. He turned and saw us and although looking a little surprised pointed to one of the long trestle tables. We sat down and a few minutes later a young girl appeared with a litre of wine and two glasses. Gradually the place started to fill up and some half-hour later we were all served wonderful thick slices of perfectly cooked pork along with roast potatoes, some mixed fresh vegetables and huge communal salads.

What I rather like about the rural Spanish is that they are hospitable, but once they see that you are settled and have everything that you want, they leave you alone to get on with their own conversation and on the whole have an apparent lack of curiosity as to why or how you are there.

The meal was delicious but on finishing and rising to pay, the chef wrote eight euros on a piece of paper. I tried to insist that it must be more but he just pointed in turn to me, then Gill, the empty wine bottle and the piece of paper. I left ten euros which still seemed ridiculous for what we had consumed. We never did find out whether it was some sort of subsidised village dinner that we had managed to gatecrash!

Continuing through the Sierra Moreno the following day, we eventually reached Hostal Guzzman at Dos Barrios in the late afternoon. On the way over I had practised asking for both a room and the cost in Spanish. Confident in my fluency, I parked and on entering the hostal, put these questions, rather like a parrot, in Spanish to the barman. He looked at me with no comprehension whatsoever but from out of the kitchen a male voice shouted, "Yes we have a room and it's forty euros, the same as he paid last time." The manager/proprietor, for it was he, later explained that with few foreigners stopping there, he remembered us from previous visits.

Avoiding Madrid and heading north, we decided to spend a few days in the Picos de Europa, somewhere we had never been before. This must be one of the most scenically beautiful areas in Spain. Forested green valleys with fast flowing rivers and high mountain ranges with snow-capped peaks, reminiscent of Switzerland. Reputedly there are both bears and wolves within the environs of the Picos, although unfortunately (or fortunately) we saw neither.

We headed for the very centre first, to a place called Fuente Dé, having followed a road along a very pretty valley from Potcs, Potcs itself being a very picturesque little town straddling a river. Fuente Dé, a small ski resort with a cable car running up to the Mirador del Cable at about six and a half thousand feet, is not so much a village as just two hotels. One is a Parador, which as I have mentioned before, we avoid, as although they are usually lovely places, they are not our idea of Spain. The other was a small family owned place, nestling in the valley with lovely views all round. Unfortunately, however, it was one of our less successful choices. It was fairly expensive, which would not have mattered had the food been better. We stayed four nights as the walking was very good (using a cable car for access) but during our sojourn there we were the only guests.

The most well-known attraction in the Picos, is probably Garganta del Cares. This is a gorge some half a kilometre in depth and which has a twelve kilometre meandering walk along its length. To reach here we drove round through Potes and Pannes and at the small town of Los Arenas, took a left turn onto the As254 to Poncebos. From here, the only driveable route is back the same way, although there is a road up into the mountains, which leads to the small village of Tielva, Sotros and finally Treviso.

A fairly new funicular from Poncebos, runs up through a mountain to what was, until recently, the isolated and inaccessible mountain village of Bulnes. Just opposite, across the river to the entrance of the funicular, we found Hostal Garganta. This was a restaurant/bar with rooms, run by a very friendly couple who spoke no English at all. After our experience in Fuenta Dé, we initially booked in for one night only. Still having two or three hours of daylight, we had a stroll along the trail through the gorge for perhaps two or three miles before returning for dinner at the hostal. What a pleasant surprise, the food was superb. My first course was two fried eggs, spicy minced beef and corn cakes, followed be a delicious goat stew with fresh vegetables and potatoes. Gill, the La Mujer, (pronounced 'moo hair') had a huge plate of giant butter beans (in a Spanish sauce) followed by chicken casserole. We accompanied this with a couple of jugs of a very palatable local (Asturias) wine. Senor then gave us a couple of glasses of Cremas de Asturias with our coffee, which Gill loved but it was too sweet for me. Spotting me giving mine to Gill, he came over with a glass of brandy which was much more to my taste.

I am very rarely sick but that night I was as sick as the proverbial dog. There was nothing wrong with the food, my gluttony was my undoing, mixing such items as fried eggs, spicy minced beef and goat stew! Gill seemed to find this highly amusing. However, having recovered the next day, we booked in for a further two nights and set off to do some walking.

Catching the first funicular up to Bulnes (no one else on it) we spent some time looking round the village which is split in two parts, higher and lower. The lower part has, with the advent of the funicular, two or three taverns and a small posada. The higher section of the village appears to be fairly derelict with only a few stone houses occupied. Although the setting of Bulnes is spectacularly beautiful, in a green valley surrounded by mountains, with a river running under an old stone bridge and some fifteen hundred feet above where we were staying, I can imagine that it would hold no attraction for young people to live there. There is no vehicular access to it at all (hence the funicular), the only other access being a steep climb up a mountain track which takes one and a half to two hours.

After having had a cup of coffee in a small bar, we followed a path towards Sotres which led up into the mountains. At some point before reaching the ridge, we were afforded a wonderful view of Naranjo de Bulnes. This mountain at 2529 metres, and with the appearance of a small Mont Blanc, is probably one of the best known climbs in Spain. Its west wall is vertical, and at five to six hundred metres high is considered 'difficult'.

Reaching the ridge, we found a small, derelict, stone cottage, so sitting in the sun against one of the walls, we had our lunch of crusty bread, serrano and tomatoes, along with some local wine. We could have been in Switzerland. We were in a perfect alpine meadow, short green grass and a plethora of wild flowers, with high, snow-capped peaks surrounding us. Our intention had been to continue down to Sotres and then to either return the same way or to follow the small road from Sotres that runs back through Tielve and eventually down to the base of the funicular, about ten miles. However, indolence carried the day, the spot was too perfect to leave in a hurry! Returning, therefore, by the track we had climbed to the ridge, we had another coffee in Bulnes and feeling a little guilty at our laziness, decided not to take the funicular back but to continue down the mountain track to the gorge. This proved to be, because of its steepness in parts, one of those paths that is probably easier to ascend than descend. In any event we were back at the hostal in an hour and a half.

Another excellent dinner! I had fabadas (a stew of pork, beans, black pudding and chorizo), Gill had veal with cheese sauce and along with a bottle of wine, we also tried some of the local sidre.

The next day being Sunday, we thought it would be nice to walk up to Bulnes and have lunch but first we would have a walk further into the gorge. It really is a spectacular path, hugging sheer cliffs to one side with a drop of several hundred feet on the other. There are one or two bridges over the river and the odd tunnel through sections of rock. On the whole the track is wide enough not to be too formidable, unless one has a real fear of heights, but at one point we did come across a landslip which stretched for some hundred metres. We walked a round trip of some six or seven miles which took about three hours. This included scrabbling about on the landslip and assisting a lunatic 'Frog' who had driven his family and a large towed caravan part of the way along the track into the mouth of the gorge!

God knows where he thought he was going; he was probably following a sat nav!

It was now about midday, so after a quick drink in our hostal bar we set off for the fifteen hundred feet climb up to Bulnes. It took us about the same time to walk up as it had to walk down the previous day. We had a very nice lunch in a small restaurant, accompanied by a feeling of smugness that one has when safe in the knowledge that because of the four to five hours of fairly strenuous exercise, the lunch calories were already spoken for! After lunch we walked back down again, more calories in the bank for dinner!

Another first class dinner, how wonderful to have found such a good cook. She (the lady owner) and Gill, after their joint greeting of 'Buenos dias' each morning, would then just look at each other and laugh, knowing this was the full extent of their communication. She really did know her rustic Spanish food and always appeared delighted at our appreciation.

One not to be forgotten, as opposed to memorable, meal at the previous hotel in Fuente Dé, was a speciality of the house. It consisted of chopped ham and chopped, tinned artichokes, quite astonishing!

A Short Rant!

I really can't stand places where the chef or cook has no idea of what they are doing, no idea of what ingredients go together, or don't, and if by chance they have managed to combine some compatible commodities, then mess them up in preparation and/or cooking. But neither am I particularly impressed with the so called 'celebrity restaurants' in this country. We ate at a well-known fish restaurant a few years ago, where all the customers appeared to be eating quietly and with what I can only describe as a sense of reverence. It lacked completely the informality and chatter that one experiences in restaurants in Spain and France and particularly Italy.

The meal was good and apart from the price, deserved no criticism but what we ate we could have eaten in a dozen restaurants in Dieppe or Jersey, or for that matter, Spain or Italy for half the price and with a far more vibrant ambience and less of a feeling of dining in the cloisters of a church!

We had asked to stay at the hostal for a further two nights, making five in all and spent the next few days exploring the area further. On our departure, Gill was presented with a bottle of Cremas de Asturias and I with a bill, which was considerably less than we had paid in Fuente Dé – two hundred and seventy-five euros in total. Needless to say, we have been back since.

It is only some forty miles along the coast from Santander to where one turns off to access the Picos. However, although there is a motorway, it is worth avoiding this and travelling along the old coast road (CA131) to Santillana. The countryside here is much like Cornwall, green low rolling terrain and almost set back in time. Even in more recent years we have seen a number of hay carts pulled by horses. Santillana is a small, medieval village with a number of very attractive stone and timber-framed cottages and several hotels and hostals. Our destination though, for our last night prior to catching the ferry, was a small hostal between Satillano and Santander. It consisted of not much more than a small bar and dining room with a few rooms above and we had stayed there previously. It was owned by a youngish man who spoke quite good English and always seemed to recognise us when we turned up. The food had always been quite good but in subsequent visits in later years (2005/2007) had gradually got worse.

Our most recent trip to Spain was in October/November of 2011. On arriving back in Santander after our six-week tour, we decided to try and find a better standard hotel or hostal, as we had two nights to wait before catching the ferry. Driving towards Santillano we saw what we thought was our usual hostal (we had not been since selling our apartment in November 2007) but weren't quite sure as something resembling a castle had been built to one side, in what had been a very large car park. Intrigued, we turned back and drove in. As I got out of the car, the young owner came out of his bar, which was still there, and asked me how I was, as if he had seen me the previous week! He explained that he and his brother had had this (four-star) hotel built in 2009. We stayed on this occasion (2011) for two nights. The rooms were of a high standard and so was the food. Our stay, including dinners, a big breakfast buffet, a few beers, two bottles of Rioja and coffees and brandies came to the princely sum of two hundred and five euros.

In 2002 our stay that last night of our tour, had cost seventy-five euros including dinner and drinks. So the extra twenty-five or so euros per night paid in 2011 was incredible value considering the gap in time and the huge difference in standards.

Arriving in Santander and having some four or five hours to wait for the ferry's departure, we parked on the quay and had a wander round the town. The ferry, which we booked in advance, was still reasonably busy even in early November. The food on board Brittany Ferries is excellent, as you would expect on a French boat. If it can be done, it is definitely worth travelling in one of their luxury or commodore cabins, as one can escape the 'hoi-poloi' if the ship is busy. Travelling in these cabins, apart from having plenty of space and seating areas and a balcony, one also has access to a private lounge. There is steward service in the cabin and priority reservations in the restaurant.

We had been away for some two and a half months, driven six and a half thousand miles at a cost of seven thousand pounds. I wonder what it would cost today.

In our travels we have met some very interesting people. We have discovered some beautiful parts of Europe and have had some wonderful experiences. Experiences that I would think are, on the whole, not possible unless one travels the way we do.

Britain's Inequalities

When one is young, and probably busily occupied working and bringing up a family, one thinks sometimes (if one thinks at all) of older people as curmudgeonly and complaining, and with less tolerance than younger people. This short piece may prove this perception to be factual or not, or even perhaps somewhere in between. An argument could be made that it is not necessarily age (young or old) which colours one's view of life in this country but the leisure time available to give it thought; and perhaps also the resignation that one assumes from hearing the same old promises and platitudes from politicians, over and over again. This is written in the weeks leading up to the general election and we are all having to re-live them. Certainly, I don't think that I ever gave a great deal of thought to the inequalities and inherent unfairness in our society, there was never time. Had I have done so however, I honestly think that my views would scarcely be dissimilar to what they are now.

I wrote this book and entitled it *The Baby Boomers* because there is (as already mentioned) a growing, rather insidious enmity towards older people. A feeling engendered and propagated by certain broadcasters, usually the BBC, and not a few politicians. An intimation and sometimes an assertion that my generation has had it easy! That we, along with bankers and a few other nefarious sections of society are the cause of the present malaise. Well, before going into their accusations, let us first take a look at the accusers, in the spirit of the aforementioned unfairness.

First, the politicians. They believe that they are underpaid and yet the ordinary 'bog standard' MP earns two and a half times the country's average salary, boosted tremendously by expenses and 'gold plated' pensions. And let us not forget, whilst on the subject of expenses, that a great number of those who stretched the bounds of moral credibility in relation to expenses, five years or so ago, are still with us. Even worse, a number of them (no longer MPs) and some convicted of various crimes, are handed out passes to enable them access to the parliamentary estate, including, of course, all the subsidised bars and restaurants.

But still the cry rings out from some of these characters, that pensioners have never had it so good – scrap the heating allowance and free bus passes. The heating allowance was brought in by the Labour government, in their usual patrician manner, in an effort to show how generous they could be with our money. It should, of course, never have been a separate entity but included in what is one of the lowest state pensions, by comparison. In a recent *Which* report, we rank number twelve out of fifteen of the richest nations. This report, incidentally, is using the new pension rates for the UK, which do not come into operation until 2016 and in any case do not apply to people who retired prior to that date. Why not, one has to ask? We have paid into the system all our working lives and no doubt a huge percentage of us are still doing so in the form of income tax, council tax and VAT etcetera. Why are we now to be the bottom tier of a two-tier system? In regard to bus passes, these can be a boon to anyone living in a rural area and no doubt of course, in town too. There may be people who do not need them, or even use them (myself included) but to try and means test them I am sure would not be worthwhile.

Finally, on politicians. I have never heard one of these characters, when pontificating on these two subjects, either mention (or be asked) about their own gold-plated pensions, or of course the fact that they are the one other section of society that is entitled to free travel.

Public Sector Pensions

Whilst on the subject of pensions, the public sector has to be brought into the equation. This is a time bomb waiting to explode in the not too distant future because of the increasing, massive liabilities of the state, i.e., the taxpayer, in regard to these entitlements. The present government, who vowed to tackle this problem, have merely tinkered with it. A cowardly lack of will on its part, when faced with the intransigence of the various unions and other interested parties.

Can anyone give a sensible reason as to why the state should be responsible for the pensions of its employees? It has become palpably obvious in recent years that employers can in no way continue to afford final salary, index-linked pensions. And yet, despite nearly all schemes having closed in the private sector, the government has backed away in the face of adversity and acceded to this merry dance towards bankruptcy.

The cost of this madness? The latest figures produced by analysts for the tax year 2016/17 is for a massive thirty-nine billion pounds and snowballing. There is something in the region of twenty per cent of the working population of the UK entitled to these extraordinary benefits, while the rest of us have to pay for them. Just recently, the Institute of Fiscal Studies said that for an average public sector worker earning twenty-seven thousand pounds per year and with an average defined benefit pension pot, tax payers are funding each pot to the tune of Four thousand eight hundred pounds per annum. Some eighty-four per cent of the public sector workers enjoy this kind of pension arrangement compared to eight per cent in the private sector and yet the present government tells us that 'We are all in this together'.

The eighty per cent not entitled to these gold-plated perks have to provide for themselves and that is much easier said than done. By far and away the majority of people employed in the private sector (some twenty-three million) have no pension provision, apart from the state pension, whatsoever. Of that twenty-three million, some three million contribute to a workplace pension (down from nine to ten million a few years ago) and six or seven million contribute to a private pension. There is nothing guaranteed about these private pensions as they are subject to the risks and vagaries of investment, and certainly in the past, to iniquitous charges and fees. The average pension pot in this sector is about twenty-seven thousand pounds, which at today's rates would purchase a paltry inflation proof annuity of some one thousand, one hundred and twenty pounds per year. When one then compares the expectations of the majority of the working population to the feather-bedding of the public sector, the problem is self-evident.

Gill and I had accumulated a pension pot of two hundred and fifty thousand pounds which had been held in cash SIPPs at five per cent interest. Our intention was to leave it there for a good number of years to come but when the recession hit and along with quantitative easing, the interest rate dropped to 0.25%, there was little point in leaving it in a cash fund. After taking twenty-five per cent tax free, we were forced into purchasing annuities which provided us with a gross income of eleven thousand three hundred pounds per annum. Does this seem reasonable? I don't think so! Furthermore, as from April 2015, we would no longer have been forced into the purchase of annuities. We have other investments but many people are not in that fortunate position.

Compare this with a letter I read recently in one of the financial sections of a newspaper. It was a query from someone working in the NHS, in regard to some private pensions he or she held, besides their NHS pension entitlement. To précis the letter, the salient point was that he or she was fifty-seven years of age, intending to retire at sixty and would receive an NHS pension in excess of fifty-five thousand pounds per year. I have no idea what this person does for a living, one suspects that the likelihood is that they are part of the management team or a consultant or GP. Whichever it is, NHS data shows that two thousand five hundred employees are on a retirement income of sixty-seven thousand pounds per annum (three quarters of them doctors) and that NHS staff with an expected pension of over fifty thousand pounds per annum represents three per cent of annual retirement but accounts for twenty-two per cent of total pension payment. This surely has to be one of the reasons for the growing shortage of GPs. Ever since Gordon Brown did as his predecessor (Nye Bevan) did and 'stuffed their mouths with gold', we have had an increasing shortage, as they appear to retire in droves. A recent survey by the BMA suggests that one third of GPs over the age of fifty, are considering retiring in the next five years. The BMA incidentally, is an organisation that in its protection of the perceived rights of its members, makes UNISON and other unions look like amateurs in their field.

GPs have been described in the past as 'gatekeepers' to the people with real knowledge. I am not sure that this is entirely fair in all cases but I have to say, no one stands on their dignity like a doctor if one questions their view.

The other side of the coin, again in the NHS, is the entitlement of our daughter, Karen, a fully qualified nurse (band six) of some fifteen years, earning twenty-eight thousand pounds per annum and expects a pension of twenty-eight thousand, lump sum, and ten thousand three hundred per year, with eligibility at sixty-five, not sixty. Furthermore, two or three years ago she had to accept a salary cut to the top of band five and has recently received a one per cent rise, the first in three years. What a disparity! Although it has to be said that millions in the private sector would be glad of a pension such as this.

Local Government Pensions

Local government pensions are another example of the ludicrous situation we are in. In England, for the tax year 2012/13, the total revenue collected in council tax was twenty-two point four billion pounds. A phenomenal five point seven billion of this was paid out in pensions, twenty-five per cent and rising. Scotland, as one would expect, was worse at approaching fifty percent. And yet, instead of trying to tackle the problem, services are being cut, 'non-jobs' are still being advertised and the only reason council tax hasn't rocketed is because it has been held in check by the present government.

Apart from a natural resistance to change, when it affects one personally, there also appears to be a total ignorance of what pension value could be achieved from the contributions made within the public sector. The level of contributions made within the police and fire brigade, to take just two, would, in a SIPPs, be unlikely to achieve forty per cent of their expected pension in the public sector.

Public sector pensions are totally unsustainable and should be scrapped for new employees and drastically revised for present staff. Forcing the public sector to take responsibility for pension provision itself, would free up billions which in turn could provide a fairer pension for all.

Finally, in regard to the public sector, whether it is the NHS, social services, the police and many other sectors, when things go wrong, sometimes catastrophically, then no one is held responsible. The usual procedure is for these individuals to be promoted, or at worst, moved sideways, or to retire, whatever the endeavours of our free (but threatened) press to gain some justice for the victims.

The BBC

This is a behemoth of overpaid managers, broadcasters and so-called talent. Salaries and benefits within this organisation make MPs look like paupers. It wouldn't matter if it wasn't public money, but it is. Call me an old cynic but is this why we have no really incisive questioning of politicians on radio and TV, in case they turn on the interviewer, pointing out their absurd salaries and entitlements? The excuse always trotted out is that it is necessary to pay the market rate. This is a nonsense. They are creating the market rate as they do not have to compete with anyone. The income of the BBC is secure and not subject to market pressures. Furthermore, I, and I am sure many viewers do not watch a particular programme because of who is presenting it (there are some I don't watch for this reason) so that when the presenter is absent, through illness or holiday say, no one misses them. Very often the 'lesser mortal' given the slot is better, more incisive, perhaps keener!

The salaries are totally unwarranted. No one in any section of the public sector, the BBC, the NHS, local government, the civil service etcetera, etcetera, should earn more than the prime minister of this country, and yet there are thousands who do.

The BBC, which should be impartial, is very often accused of left wing bias and anyone who listens or watches political programmes, interviews or, in some cases, reported news items, cannot help but agree. The old maxim 'If you are not a socialist when you are twenty, then you have no heart. But if you are still a socialist at forty, then you have no brain', apparently carries little weight in this organisation!

There are one or two interviewers who, whatever their political leanings, I feel are quite even handed, but they are few and far between.

I have digressed a little from my main complaint in regard to the BBC. This was, of course, the prejudice against older people and the ridiculous salaries and benefits paid in the main for jobs that with a couple of weeks training, hundreds of thousands of people would be capable of. In regard to the prejudice, I caught the tail end of an interview in the business section of the *Today* programme at about 6.30 am just recently. In this, the interviewer, (whose name I don't know) was discussing the imminent release of the new pension bonds. This interviewer, who I assume was an economist, or at least had some business training of some sort, pressed his interviewee over and over again to agree with his opinion that these bonds amounted to young people subsidising older people. It was obvious that the person being interviewed did not agree with him, but he pursued it until he realised that his slot had run out of time.

I have heard the term 'generational theft' used and more recently I watched an interview with the Chancellor, where it was suggested that the new bonds were over-generous and probably being subsidised, as a bribe to older voters. Quite obviously, any government running towards a general election will view 'sweeteners', where possible, as a good idea, it would be naïve not to do so. However, the interest rates on these bonds of two point eight percent and four percent, only appear generous against current low yield investments. Why is this? Because other rates paid have been reduced through quantitative easing and a low base rate, to a virtual non-return after inflation is taken into account; whilst mortgages are at an all-time low, so benefitting younger people wishing to buy a home. This could be construed as generational theft too, but not of course in the same direction as that propagated by the denizens of the BBC.

Furthermore, let's take a look at the rates paid on the bonds. The funds (billions) that the government will raise could be borrowed at a lesser rate – two per cent I believe. However, when the interest is paid, being taxable, it will be immediately discounted by twenty per cent –

two point eight per cent becoming two point two four per cent and four per cent becoming three point two per cent. Pensioners will no doubt spend some or all of this extra income, so producing a further boost to the economy. Meanwhile the government has these extra funds available for investment. Certainly when I was in business, I would have been glad of the opportunity to borrow at four per cent, particularly with the benefit of the aforementioned discount on repayment!

So to Sum Up.

I do not pretend that my generation was 'hard done by', in fact at the beginning of this book I mention that we were the lucky generation. However, we did work for what we have and some of us, sometimes, extremely hard. We expected nothing from anyone, no hand-outs, no dole, no benefits and certainly in our case, didn't get any. To have been out of work and receive benefits was viewed as undignified and I am sure that many people who are in that unfortunate position today would see it in the same way. However, there are many that do not and appear to view it as a right, a lifestyle choice and not just the safety net that it is supposed to be.

Who then are the villains of the piece, if not the pensioners? They are myriad, some already mentioned but we may as well list most of them.

There are the bankers who came close to wrecking the country and who not only have not been penalised but continue to draw the excessive salaries and bonuses to which they believe they are entitled. And although they have drawn millions over the last few years (what recession?) our shares in RBS are still down ninety-one per cent on the purchase cost.

Politicians, the BBC, public sector pensions (including local government) have all been addressed.

Immigration, by the millions, since the millennium. This has not only created overload in our hospitals, GP surgeries, education and housing but has held down wages. Labour's (who were responsible for the huge increase in immigration) answer to this was to introduce tax credits. One would think a curious policy for a socialist government, i.e., to subsidise private enterprise with public funds. But of course, socialists always know how best to spend our money for us, and of course there is always the expectation that most immigrants will vote Labour.

Any business should be capable of paying a living wage to its employees. If it is not, then it is not viable and if it is, it is being handed state funding unnecessarily. In either case there should be no funding of this nature available at all.

If the Conservatives believe in private enterprise, this ridiculous form of subsidy should have been stopped long ago.

Firms and wealthy individuals who do not pay their fair share of tax. Where tax evasion takes place, the law is there to deal with it – use it! Tax avoidance should be looked at more critically. It is no use politicians grandstanding and criticising firms who are legitimately (not by legerdemain) not paying what is perceived to be a fair amount of tax. Do something about it! Change the law and tie up the loopholes. Difficult probably but surely not beyond the wit of the treasury.

Welfare

Where does one start?

Sickness and incapacity benefit. Two point five million claimants receiving thirteen billion per annum. Does anyone truly believe there are two point five million people incapable of work in this country? The latest assessment is that some forty to forty-five per cent are capable of working and therefore not entitled to the benefits they are receiving.

Over five million working age benefit claimants.

Two point two five million pension credit claimants.
Four hundred and seventy-five thousand lone parents claiming income support.
Four point nine three million claiming housing benefit.

Property

Council property sold off and not replaced, so along with immigration creating a shortage of properties to rent. The consequences? Ever higher rents that people cannot afford without the help of housing benefit and tax credits.

Council Tax

Already touched on but this illogical tax is worse than VAT. VAT obviously affects the less well off more than the wealthy, but can be circumvented by just not purchasing anything! Council tax however, falls into bands but with no upper limit for band H, the highest band. This means, in reality, that someone living in a property worth millions, will only pay three times more than someone in a bedsit, which falls into band A. Unlike VAT, there is no escape unless you take to a tent!

Overseas Aid

Almost twelve billion pounds handed out in our name (but without the majority's consent, just to make 'grandstanding politicians' feel good. Millions handed to countries, sufficiently wealthy (whatever their poverty) to operate their own space projects and in other cases, to arm themselves to the teeth, very often, one might add, to subjugate their own people. Many of these states incidentally, although giving the appearance of being friendly towards Britain, are in fact intensely hostile.

Charities

Granted millions of pounds in state funding and where the senior staff are again on salaries far in excess of the prime minister's.

Quangos, the House of Lords, part time public sector placements – I could go on, but do I need to? I think the point has been made.

So, younger generation, perhaps we (the older generation) are not the culprits, the blame may lie elsewhere. Perhaps there are just too many snouts in the trough!